WOJCIECH JARUZELSKI

WORLD LEADERS   PAST & PRESENT

WOJCIECH JARUZELSKI

Lynn Berry

CHELSEA HOUSE PUBLISHERS
NEW YORK
PHILADELPHIA

Chelsea House Publishers
EDITOR-IN-CHIEF: Nancy Toff
EXECUTIVE EDITOR: Remmel T. Nunn
MANAGING EDITOR: Karyn Gullen Browne
COPY CHIEF: Juliann Barbato
PICTURE EDITOR: Adrian G. Allen
ART DIRECTOR: Maria Epes
MANUFACTURING MANAGER: Gerald Levine

World Leaders—Past & Present
SENIOR EDITOR: John W. Selfridge

Staff for WOJCIECH JARUZELSKI
COPY EDITOR: Karen Hammonds
DEPUTY COPY CHIEF: Mark Rifkin
EDITORIAL ASSISTANT: Nate Eaton
PICTURE RESEARCHER: Andrea Reithmayr
ASSISTANT ART DIRECTOR: Loraine Machlin
DESIGNER: James Baker
PRODUCTION MANAGER: Joseph Romano
PRODUCTION COORDINATOR: Marie Claire Cebrián
COVER ILLUSTRATION: Bryn Barnard

Copyright © 1990 Chelsea House Publishers, a division of Main Line Book Co. All rights reserved. Printed and bound in the United States of America.

First Printing

1 3 5 7 9 8 6 4 2

Library of Congress Cataloging-in-Publication Data

Berry, Lynn.
  Wojciech Jaruzelski/Lynn Berry.
  p. cm.—(World leaders past & present)
  Includes bibliographical references.
  Summary: An illustrated biography of the Polish leader.
  ISBN 1-55546-838-1
       0-7910-0677-8 (pbk.)
  1. Jaruzelski, W. (Wojciech)—Juvenile literature. 2. Heads of state—Poland—Biography—Juvenile literature. [1. Jaruzelski, W. (Wojciech) 2. Heads of state.] I. Title. II. Series.
DK4435.J37B47   1990
943.805'6'092—dc20   89–71191
[B]   CIP
[92]   AC

Contents

"On Leadership," Arthur M. Schlesinger, jr.	7
1. State of War	13
2. A Polish Patriot	25
3. A Boy in History	35
4. The Fascist Menace	45
5. The Face of Communism	55
6. The Thaw	67
7. The Cycle of Unrest	79
8. Hard Work and Perseverance	93
Further Reading	108
Chronology	109
Index	110

WORLD LEADERS　　PAST & PRESENT

John Adams
John Quincy Adams
Konrad Adenauer
Alexander the Great
Salvador Allende
Marc Antony
Corazon Aquino
Yasir Arafat
King Arthur
Hafez al-Assad
Kemal Atatürk
Attila
Clement Attlee
Augustus Caesar
Menachem Begin
David Ben-Gurion
Otto von Bismarck
Léon Blum
Simón Bolívar
Cesare Borgia
Willy Brandt
Leonid Brezhnev
Julius Caesar
John Calvin
Jimmy Carter
Fidel Castro
Catherine the Great
Charlemagne
Chiang Kai-Shek
Winston Churchill
Georges Clemenceau
Cleopatra
Constantine the Great
Hernán Cortés
Oliver Cromwell
Georges-Jacques Danton
Jefferson Davis
Moshe Dayan
Charles de Gaulle
Eamon De Valera
Eugene Debs
Deng Xiaoping
Benjamin Disraeli
Alexander Dubček
François & Jean-Claude Duvalier
Dwight Eisenhower
Eleanor of Aquitaine
Elizabeth I
Faisal
Ferdinand & Isabella
Francisco Franco
Benjamin Franklin

Frederick the Great
Indira Gandhi
Mohandas Gandhi
Giuseppe Garibaldi
Amin & Bashir Gemayel
Genghis Khan
William Gladstone
Mikhail Gorbachev
Ulysses S. Grant
Ernesto "Che" Guevara
Tenzin Gyatso
Alexander Hamilton
Dag Hammarskjöld
Henry VIII
Henry of Navarre
Paul von Hindenburg
Hirohito
Adolf Hitler
Ho Chi Minh
King Hussein
Ivan the Terrible
Andrew Jackson
James I
Wojciech Jaruzelski
Thomas Jefferson
Joan of Arc
Pope John XXIII
Pope John Paul II
Lyndon Johnson
Benito Juárez
John Kennedy
Robert Kennedy
Jomo Kenyatta
Ayatollah Khomeini
Nikita Khrushchev
Kim Il Sung
Martin Luther King, Jr.
Henry Kissinger
Kublai Khan
Lafayette
Robert E. Lee
Vladimir Lenin
Abraham Lincoln
David Lloyd George
Louis XIV
Martin Luther
Judas Maccabeus
James Madison
Nelson & Winnie Mandela
Mao Zedong
Ferdinand Marcos
George Marshall

Mary, Queen of Scots
Tomáš Masaryk
Golda Meir
Klemens von Metternich
James Monroe
Hosni Mubarak
Robert Mugabe
Benito Mussolini
Napoléon Bonaparte
Gamal Abdel Nasser
Jawaharlal Nehru
Nero
Nicholas II
Richard Nixon
Kwame Nkrumah
Daniel Ortega
Mohammed Reza Pahlavi
Thomas Paine
Charles Stewart Parnell
Pericles
Juan Perón
Peter the Great
Pol Pot
Muammar el-Qaddafi
Ronald Reagan
Cardinal Richelieu
Maximilien Robespierre
Eleanor Roosevelt
Franklin Roosevelt
Theodore Roosevelt
Anwar Sadat
Haile Selassie
Prince Sihanouk
Jan Smuts
Joseph Stalin
Sukarno
Sun Yat-sen
Tamerlane
Mother Teresa
Margaret Thatcher
Josip Broz Tito
Toussaint L'Ouverture
Leon Trotsky
Pierre Trudeau
Harry Truman
Queen Victoria
Lech Walesa
George Washington
Chaim Weizmann
Woodrow Wilson
Xerxes
Emiliano Zapata
Zhou Enlai

CHELSEA HOUSE PUBLISHERS

ON LEADERSHIP

Arthur M. Schlesinger, jr.

LEADERSHIP, it may be said, is really what makes the world go round. Love no doubt smooths the passage; but love is a private transaction between consenting adults. Leadership is a public transaction with history. The idea of leadership affirms the capacity of individuals to move, inspire, and mobilize masses of people so that they act together in pursuit of an end. Sometimes leadership serves good purposes, sometimes bad; but whether the end is benign or evil, great leaders are those men and women who leave their personal stamp on history.

Now, the very concept of leadership implies the proposition that individuals can make a difference. This proposition has never been universally accepted. From classical times to the present day, eminent thinkers have regarded individuals as no more than the agents and pawns of larger forces, whether the gods and goddesses of the ancient world or, in the modern era, race, class, nation, the dialectic, the will of the people, the spirit of the times, history itself. Against such forces, the individual dwindles into insignificance.

So contends the thesis of historical determinism. Tolstoy's great novel *War and Peace* offers a famous statement of the case. Why, Tolstoy asked, did millions of men in the Napoleonic Wars, denying their human feelings and their common sense, move back and forth across Europe slaughtering their fellows? "The war," Tolstoy answered, "was bound to happen simply because it was bound to happen." All prior history predetermined it. As for leaders, they, Tolstoy said, "are but the labels that serve to give a name to an end and, like labels, they have the least possible connection with the event." The greater the leader, "the more conspicuous the inevitability and the predestination of every act he commits." The leader, said Tolstoy, is "the slave of history."

Determinism takes many forms. Marxism is the determinism of class. Nazism the determinism of race. But the idea of men and women as the slaves of history runs athwart the deepest human instincts. Rigid determinism abolishes the idea of human freedom—

the assumption of free choice that underlies every move we make, every word we speak, every thought we think. It abolishes the idea of human responsibility, since it is manifestly unfair to reward or punish people for actions that are by definition beyond their control. No one can live consistently by any deterministic creed. The Marxist states prove this themselves by their extreme susceptibility to the cult of leadership.

More than that, history refutes the idea that individuals make no difference. In December 1931 a British politician crossing Park Avenue in New York City between 76th and 77th Streets around 10:30 P.M. looked in the wrong direction and was knocked down by an automobile—a moment, he later recalled, of a man aghast, a world aglare: "I do not understand why I was not broken like an eggshell or squashed like a gooseberry." Fourteen months later an American politician, sitting in an open car in Miami, Florida, was fired on by an assassin; the man beside him was hit. Those who believe that individuals make no difference to history might well ponder whether the next two decades would have been the same had Mario Constasino's car killed Winston Churchill in 1931 and Giuseppe Zangara's bullet killed Franklin Roosevelt in 1933. Suppose, in addition, that Adolf Hitler had been killed in the street fighting during the Munich *Putsch* of 1923 and that Lenin had died of typhus during World War I. What would the 20th century be like now?

For better or for worse, individuals do make a difference. "The notion that a people can run itself and its affairs anonymously," wrote the philosopher William James, "is now well known to be the silliest of absurdities. Mankind does nothing save through initiatives on the part of inventors, great or small, and imitation by the rest of us—these are the sole factors in human progress. Individuals of genius show the way, and set the patterns, which common people then adopt and follow."

Leadership, James suggests, means leadership in thought as well as in action. In the long run, leaders in thought may well make the greater difference to the world. But, as Woodrow Wilson once said, "Those only are leaders of men, in the general eye, who lead in action. . . . It is at their hands that new thought gets its translation into the crude language of deeds." Leaders in thought often invent in solitude and obscurity, leaving to later generations the tasks of imitation. Leaders in action—the leaders portrayed in this series—have to be effective in their own time.

And they cannot be effective by themselves. They must act in response to the rhythms of their age. Their genius must be adapted, in a phrase of William James's, "to the receptivities of the moment." Leaders are useless without followers. "There goes the mob," said the French politician hearing a clamor in the streets. "I am their leader. I must follow them." Great leaders turn the inchoate emotions of the mob to purposes of their own. They seize on the opportunities of their time, the hopes, fears, frustrations, crises, potentialities. They succeed when events have prepared the way for them, when the community is awaiting to be aroused, when they can provide the clarifying and organizing ideas. Leadership ignites the circuit between the individual and the mass and thereby alters history.

It may alter history for better or for worse. Leaders have been responsible for the most extravagant follies and most monstrous crimes that have beset suffering humanity. They have also been vital in such gains as humanity has made in individual freedom, religious and racial tolerance, social justice, and respect for human rights.

There is no sure way to tell in advance who is going to lead for good and who for evil. But a glance at the gallery of men and women in *World Leaders—Past and Present* suggests some useful tests.

One test is this: Do leaders lead by force or by persuasion? By command or by consent? Through most of history leadership was exercised by the divine right of authority. The duty of followers was to defer and to obey. "Theirs not to reason why / Theirs but to do and die." On occasion, as with the so-called enlightened despots of the 18th century in Europe, absolutist leadership was animated by humane purposes. More often, absolutism nourished the passion for domination, land, gold, and conquest and resulted in tyranny.

The great revolution of modern times has been the revolution of equality. The idea that all people should be equal in their legal condition has undermined the old structure of authority, hierarchy, and deference. The revolution of equality has had two contrary effects on the nature of leadership. For equality, as Alexis de Tocqueville pointed out in his great study *Democracy in America*, might mean equality in servitude as well as equality in freedom.

"I know of only two methods of establishing equality in the political world," Tocqueville wrote. "Rights must be given to every citizen, or none at all to anyone . . . save one, who is the master of all." There was no middle ground "between the sovereignty of all and the absolute power of one man." In his astonishing prediction of 20th-century totalitarian dictatorship, Tocqueville explained how the revolution of equality could lead to the *"Führerprinzip"* and more terrible absolutism than the world had ever known.

But when rights are given to every citizen and the sovereignty of all is established, the problem of leadership takes a new form, becomes more exacting than ever before. It is easy to issue commands and enforce them by the rope and the stake, the concentration camp and the *gulag*. It is much harder to use argument and achievement to overcome opposition and win consent. The Founding Fathers of the United States understood the difficulty. They believed that history had given them the opportunity to decide, as Alexander Hamilton wrote in the first Federalist Paper, whether men are indeed capable of basing government on "reflection and choice, or whether they are forever destined to depend . . . on accident and force."

Government by reflection and choice called for a new style of leadership and a new quality of followership. It required leaders to be responsive to popular concerns, and it required followers to be active and informed participants in the process. Democracy does not eliminate emotion from politics; sometimes it fosters demagoguery; but it is confident that, as the greatest of democratic leaders put it, you cannot fool all of the people all of the time. It measures leadership by results and retires those who overreach or falter or fail.

It is true that in the long run despots are measured by results too. But they can postpone the day of judgment, sometimes indefinitely, and in the meantime they can do infinite harm. It is also true that democracy is no guarantee of virtue and intelligence in government, for the voice of the people is not necessarily the voice of God. But democracy, by assuring the right of opposition, offers built-in resistance to the evils inherent in absolutism. As the theologian Reinhold Niebuhr summed it up, "Man's capacity for justice makes democracy possible, but man's inclination to injustice makes democracy necessary."

A second test for leadership is the end for which power is sought. When leaders have as their goal the supremacy of a master race or the promotion of totalitarian revolution or the acquisition and exploitation of colonies or the protection of greed and privilege or the preservation of personal power, it is likely that their leadership will do little to advance the cause of humanity. When their goal is the abolition of slavery, the liberation of women, the enlargement of opportunity for the poor and powerless, the extension of equal rights to racial minorities, the defense of the freedoms of expression and opposition, it is likely that their leadership will increase the sum of human liberty and welfare.

Leaders have done great harm to the world. They have also conferred great benefits. You will find both sorts in this series. Even "good" leaders must be regarded with a certain wariness. Leaders are not demigods; they put on their trousers one leg after another just like ordinary mortals. No leader is infallible, and every leader needs to be reminded of this at regular intervals. Irreverence irritates leaders but is their salvation. Unquestioning submission corrupts leaders and demeans followers. Making a cult of a leader is always a mistake. Fortunately hero worship generates its own antidote. "Every hero," said Emerson, "becomes a bore at last."

The signal benefit the great leaders confer is to embolden the rest of us to live according to our own best selves, to be active, insistent, and resolute in affirming our own sense of things. For great leaders attest to the reality of human freedom against the supposed inevitabilities of history. And they attest to the wisdom and power that may lie within the most unlikely of us, which is why Abraham Lincoln remains the supreme example of great leadership. A great leader, said Emerson, exhibits new possibilities to all humanity. "We feed on genius. . . . Great men exist that there may be greater men."

Great leaders, in short, justify themselves by emancipating and empowering their followers. So humanity struggles to master its destiny, remembering with Alexis de Tocqueville: "It is true that around every man a fatal circle is traced beyond which he cannot pass; but within the wide verge of that circle he is powerful and free; as it is with man, so with communities."

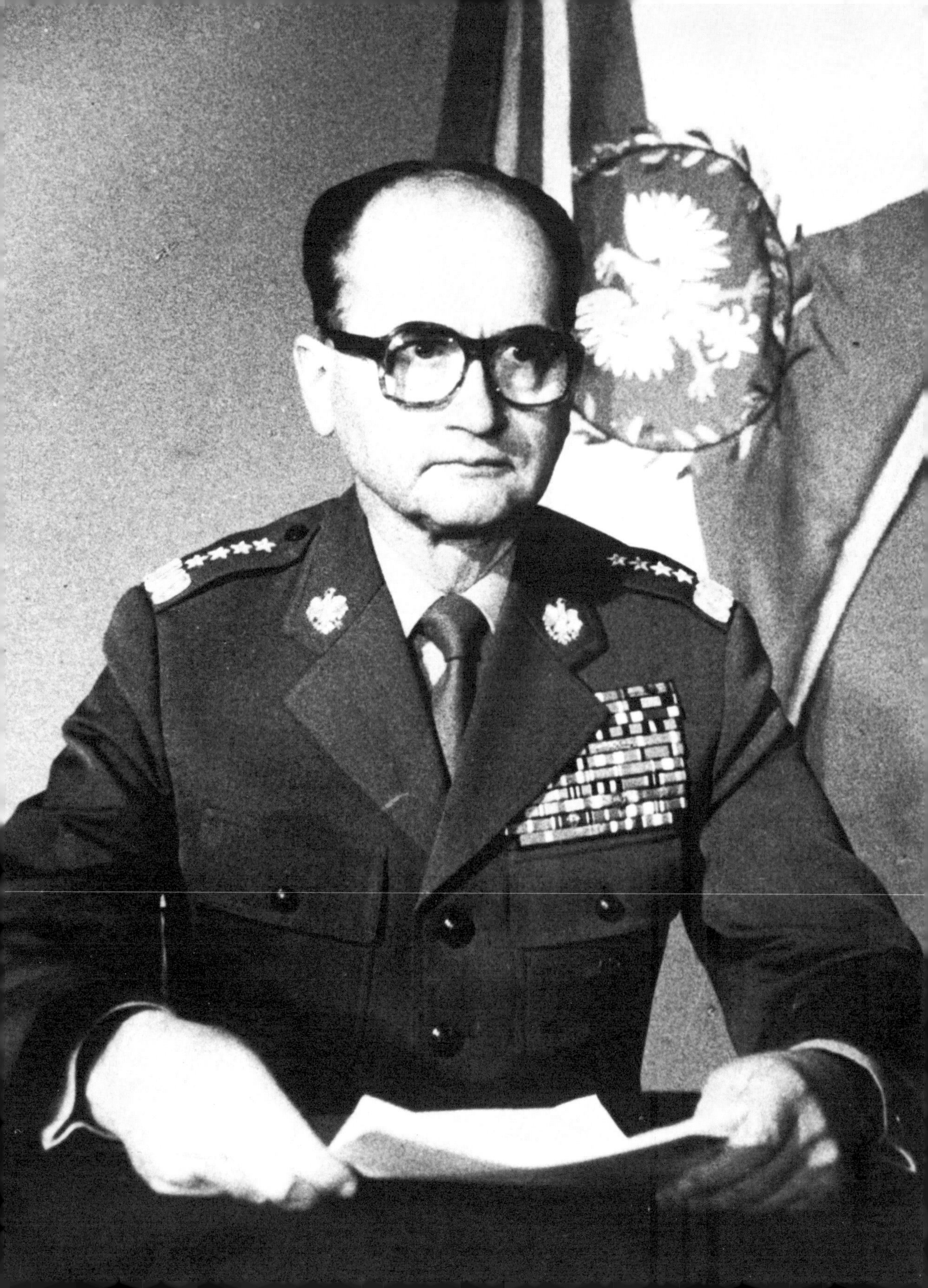

1
State of War

At midnight, on December 13, 1981, General Wojciech Jaruzelski, defense minister, prime minister, and new first secretary of the country's ruling Communist party, imposed martial law in Poland. Tanks rolled into Warsaw, Poland's capital city, and soldiers were positioned on street corners. The Polish army occupied Poland. Thousands of Polish citizens were dragged out of their beds in the middle of the night and taken to internment camps. Jaruzelski also took steps to seal off communication channels within Poland as well as those linking it with the outside world: Roadblocks were set up in and around all major cities, telephone and telegraph lines were cut, and the borders were closed.

When Poles awoke that cold Sunday morning to tanks on their city's streets, dead telephones, and news that their neighbors had been arrested, they turned on their radios and televisions hoping for an explanation. General Jaruzelski, sitting in full uniform in front of the Polish flag, delivered a speech that was broadcast repeatedly throughout the day. The expressionless, straight-backed general an-

> *The burden of responsibility which falls upon me at this dramatic moment is great. It is my duty to shoulder this responsibility, for what is at stake is the future of Poland. . . . In conformity with the provisions of the Constitution . . . the Council of State proclaimed martial law throughout the country.*
> —WOJCIECH JARUZELSKI declaring martial law, via televised and radio broadcasts, December 13, 1981

General Wojciech Jaruzelski declares martial law in Poland on national television, in December 1981. Jaruzelski believed the desperate measure was necessary to save Poland from social and economic collapse; some believe that the threat of Soviet intervention influenced his decision.

nounced that the Polish government had declared martial law (more literally translated in Polish as "state of war") in order to save the depressed Polish economy. Stores were all but empty, except for dusty bottles of vinegar. Meat, butter, flour, and sugar were rationed, but even so they rarely appeared in stores and when they did, long lines formed immediately, stretching outside the door and down the street. Military rule, he went on, was the only way to prevent the ultimate destruction of the state itself. Jaruzelski took responsibility for the decision, and most Poles hated him for it.

Jaruzelski had declared martial law to crush Solidarity. Many of the Poles arrested during the night were members or supporters of Solidarity, the first independent labor union in the Soviet bloc. Solidarity, actually a federation of free labor unions, claimed the membership of 10 million Poles and the loyalty of many more in a nation of 37 million. Founded in August 1980 during a strike at the Lenin Shipyard in Gdansk, Solidarity had become an unprecedented national movement for freedom and independence. The 16 months of Solidarity were a time of openness: Artists and scholars dared to challenge the views of the Communist government in books and films, while newspapers and television, previously under tight government control, became relatively open forums for public discussion. Poles were no longer afraid to express their opinions, and a sense of excitement filled the country as people united in a struggle for better working conditions, a voice in public policy decisions, and greater individual freedom. Then, when Jaruzelski imposed martial law and suppressed Solidarity, he dashed the Polish people's hope for a better life.

During the "state of war," Jaruzelski authorized the arrest of many people, including respected artists and intellectuals, and issued 20 decrees to bring the rest of society under control. The martial-law decrees suspended basic civil rights such as freedom of the press, freedom of speech, and freedom of assembly. All public gatherings, except church services, were banned. It was illegal to distribute printed material or even to use printing equipment,

> *All humanity's desire for peace argues for the end of martial law in Poland.*
> —POPE JOHN PAUL II
> in a letter to Jaruzelski,
> December 18, 1981

including office copying machines, without prior government approval. The martial-law decrees controlled communication even further by giving the government the right to censor mail and listen in on telephone conversations once these services were resumed. All schools and universities were closed temporarily. A strict curfew made it illegal to be on the streets between 10:00 P.M. and 6:00 A.M. Under martial law, anyone thought to threaten the interests of the state could be immediately interned for an indefinite period of time, while anyone who violated the martial-law decrees could be tried in court, with penalties ranging from heavy fines to imprisonment. Jaruzelski jailed numerous Solidarity leaders, declared the union illegal, and drove its activities underground.

Jaruzelski has said he has no regrets about his decision to impose martial law in Poland in December 1981. He claims that the economic crisis in his country was so severe and discontent so widespread that drastic measures were necessary to restore order. Although Jaruzelski never said so outright, he strongly implied that he declared martial law to save the country from Soviet military intervention. The

Polish tanks roll into Warsaw, Poland's capital, in 1981. Under martial law, the Polish military presence in Polish cities was intensified, countless citizens were arrested, and communication channels, both within the country and with the outside world, were blocked by the government.

Soviet navy was holding war games in the Baltic Sea off Poland's shores, and troops were converging on Poland's borders. Although it was not clear how real the threat was, and reason pointed against Soviet soldiers marching into Poland, the Soviet army had invaded other bloc countries in similar situations. Soviet tanks rolled into Hungary in 1956 and Czechoslovakia in 1968 to put down social unrest, prevent liberalization, and keep loyal Communist governments in power. By imposing martial law, Jaruzelski may have prevented such an invasion.

Did martial law save Poland, as Jaruzelski believes it did, from economic ruin, civil war, and the horror of a Soviet invasion? Or was there a way for him to revive the economy and restore social accord without declaring war on his own country? Did he really believe he was acting in the best interest of his country and people or was he simply following the orders of his bosses in the Kremlin? The Soviet leaders, who clearly were more interested in preserving Communist power than in helping the Poles, pressured the Polish leaders throughout 1981 to crack down on Solidarity. At the center of the issue is Jaruzelski himself and whether he is a Polish patriot, a Soviet underling, or some mixture of the two.

By persistent intimidation, Jaruzelski successfully limited open public support for Solidarity, and as the years went by fewer and fewer people heeded Solidarity's calls for strikes and demonstrations. Still, he could not destroy the Poles' loyalty to Soli-

Polish women sing their support for Solidarity. Founded in August 1980, Solidarity was the first independent trade union in Poland, but its name soon became synonymous with a national movement in Poland aimed at achieving a more participatory government and better working conditions for the country's laborers.

darity and to the ideals it represented; nor could he win the confidence of the Polish people, who refused to accept his Communist regime as the legitimate government of Poland. Compounding Jaruzelski's problems was his government's failure to reverse the economic decline and raise Poles' standard of living. The economic crisis worsened during the mid-1980s, and by 1988 strikes were again breaking out throughout Poland. The country was threatened with a new wave of social unrest that many feared would once again result in violent government suppression.

Then, to the great surprise of Poles and many in the international community, Jaruzelski acknowledged that he needed Solidarity's help both to calm the dissatisfied workers and to turn the Polish economy around. Solidarity, unlike the Communist party, had the support of the people, and Jaruzelski

The Polish military stands its ground before a Solidarity demonstration during martial law. Public demonstrations such as this, never encouraged in Poland, were totally banned by the government in December 1981.

17

Poles demonstrate on the streets of Kraków to protest food shortages and economic decline in August 1981. The numerous marches and workers' strikes in 1980–81 reflected the widespread discontent in Poland during the period leading up to the imposition of martial law.

hoped the union's leaders could convince Poles to back his government's proposed economic reforms. The reforms would involve austerity measures that for a time would make life even more difficult for many people. Everyone knew the reforms were absolutely necessary to reverse Poland's economic decline: Food prices needed to go up to encourage farmers to produce more pork and beef, and unprofitable factories needed to be closed. The latter meant that some workers would be, at least temporarily, unemployed. Jaruzelski realized that Poles would be unwilling to make these sacrifices for a government they considered incompetent and duplicitous, but he suspected they might support a reform program that was implemented by a democratically elected government. He also came to accept that some sort of reconciliation with Solidarity was going to be necessary.

Jaruzelski allowed Solidarity to emerge as a legal political opposition in 1989. The first free parliamentary elections in Eastern Europe since World War II were held in Poland on June 4 of that year, and the Communist party received a resounding defeat. Even candidates who ran unopposed on the party ticket lost. Solidarity won 99 of the 100 seats in a newly created senate and all of the 161 seats it was entitled to hold in the lower house of the Sejm, or parliament. The Senate — the upper house of parliament — was created as the result of roundtable talks between the government and Solidarity in early 1989. Elections to the Senate were fully democratic, while Solidarity was entitled to put up candidates for 161 of the 460 seats in the Assembly, the lower house of the Polish parliament.

A new, powerful presidency was also created as a result of accords signed between the party and Solidarity after the roundtable talks. Until then, the first secretary of the party had been the nation's leader. The government, headed by a prime minister, was subordinate to the party. The chairman of the Council of State, a collective presidency, was a largely ceremonial position.

The new post of president was intended to be filled by General Jaruzelski, who was elected by both houses of the Sejm on July 19. The man who declared war on his own citizens to defend autocratic Communist rule was elected the first president in what had become a multiparty state. However, for Jaruzelski it was not a fairy tale come true. He won by only one vote, and the voting was carefully orchestrated to ensure his election in light of opposition from both Solidarity delegates and delegates of smaller parties who had been loyal members of a Communist-led coalition.

The formal name of the Communist party in Poland is the Polish United Workers party. The word *communist* was conspicuously left out of the official name in an attempt to appeal to a society that is historically anti-Communist. For simplicity's sake, the party will be referred to here as the Communist party. The Peasant party and Democratic party had been part of a Communist-led coalition in parliament and in past years had obediently followed the Communist line, but their members' opposition to Jaruzelski in the presidential election and willingness to join with Solidarity delegates to form a government suggest they will act more independently in the future.

> *It was a very dramatic decision. But the farther we are from that date, the more I am convinced that [imposing martial law] was necessary. . . . All of Europe, perhaps even the whole world, could have been ignited.*
> —WOJCIECH JARUZELSKI
> 1986

Jaruzelski meets with Polish soldiers in December 1981. The prospect of Poles firing on Poles was abhorrent to Polish citizens, but when Jaruzelski declared martial law and ordered the Polish army to quell Solidarity demonstrations, precisely that potential for bloodshed was created.

Jaruzelski, the only candidate for president, received 270 of the 537 valid votes cast, the minimum needed to win under election rules that defined a majority as 50 percent plus 1. Only 1 Solidarity delegate voted for Jaruzelski, while 18 abstained and thus assured the general's election without having to vote for him themselves. Some Solidarity leaders wanted to see Jaruzelski elected. They had come to respect him, and they believed his election would appease Soviet and Polish hard-liners who might feel threatened by the sudden democratization. The overwhelming majority of Solidarity's delegates, unable to forgive Jaruzelski for the imposition of martial law nearly 10 years before, voted against him.

Jaruzelski has been a loyal Communist soldier, and as such he owes allegiance to the Soviet Union. In 1943, when Jaruzelski was only 20 years old, he attended a Soviet officers' school not far from Moscow and then joined a Polish army under Soviet command that helped liberate Poland from the Nazi Germans at the end of World War II. He stayed in the army and in the immediate postwar years took part in brutal battles against his countrymen who resisted the Communist takeover. He joined the Communist party in 1947, and his rapid rise through the ranks showed that he was trusted by party leaders in Poland and the Soviet Union. He was defense minister in 1968, when Polish troops joined the Soviet-led invasion of Czechoslovakia.

On the other hand, Jaruzelski claims the birthright of a Polish patriot, and he has reason to dislike the Soviets. He was born into a family in which the men traditionally fought against the Russians for the freedom of Poland. He attended a prestigious Catholic school until his studies were interrupted when World War II broke out and the Soviets deported him and his family to a Siberian labor camp.

Jaruzelski has been an enigma to his own people. When he appears in public he often seems stiff and expressionless, his eyes usually hidden behind dark glasses. He makes few casual remarks and prefers to read from carefully prepared texts. Jaruzelski always stands very erect when appearing in public, and this has prompted his countrymen to speculate that he wears a brace to support a weak back or compensate for a war injury. However, the general, who has been in the army since 1943, said he simply prefers the military posture. For years after he be-

The Solidarity spokesman Lech Walesa (left) and the labor mediator Tadeusz Masowiecki (center) lead a Solidarity demonstration in 1988. That year, the labor union and the government reached a general agreement to cooperate on an agenda for the improvement of working and living conditions in Poland.

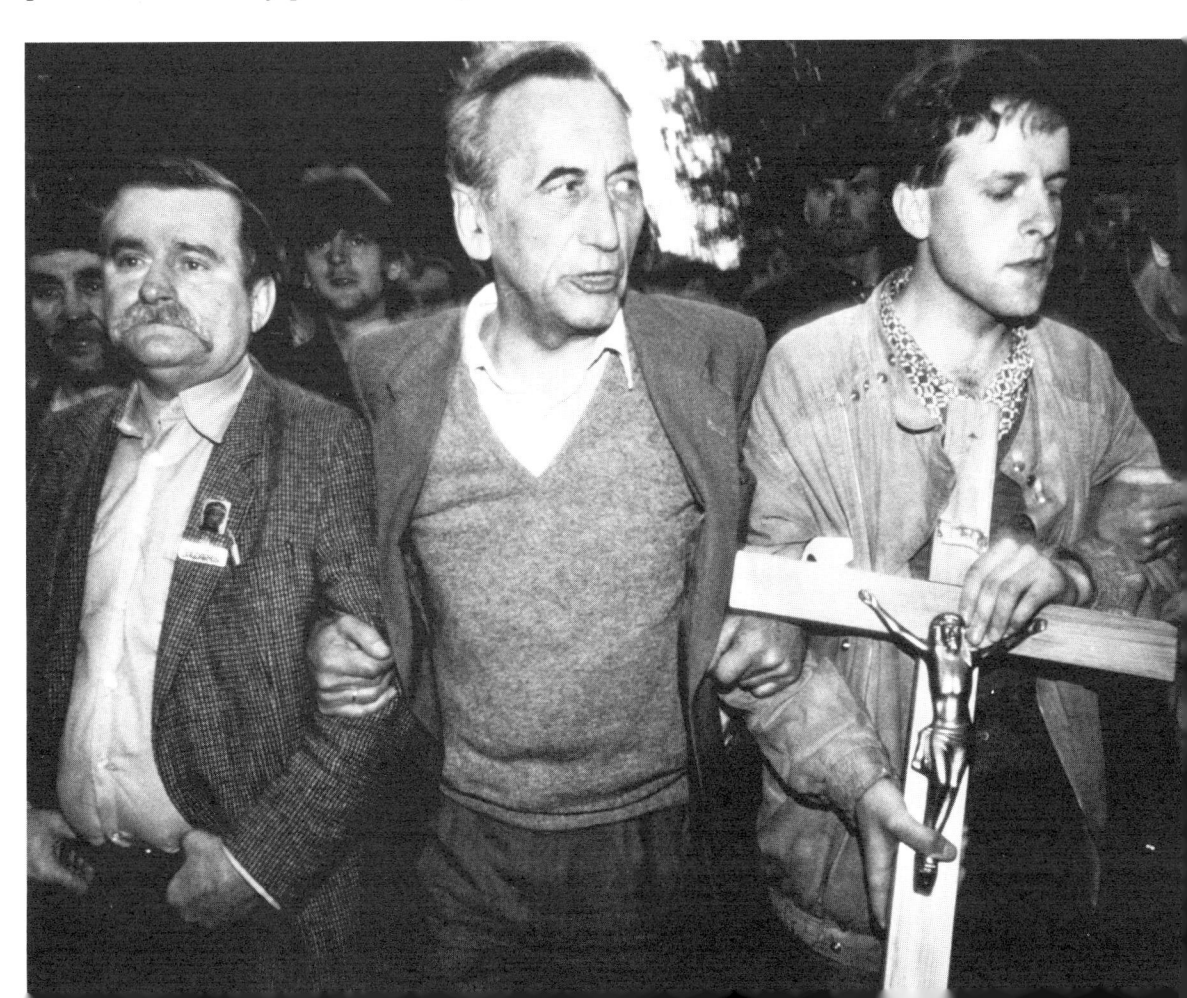

came prime minister in February 1981, he continued to wear his well-decorated military uniform to official functions. He switched to wearing a civilian suit when he ended his tenure as prime minister and became the chairman of the Council of State in November 1985.

In a more relaxed setting, however, Jaruzelski presents a somewhat different image. (The author met with Jaruzelski privately in 1988.) He is quiet, unassuming, and personable. He has the manners and graces of a well-bred nobleman, and often kisses women's hands in the old Polish tradition. His family background and his education are also reflected in his proper Polish speech. Jaruzelski often quotes from 19th-century literature and poetry, preferring the romantic verses of the Polish poet Adam Mickiewicz to the doctrines of Lenin, the Soviet founder.

The dark glasses Jaruzelski wears are not part of an affectation but are a result of the time he spent in the Siberian labor camp during World War II. His eyes were damaged by sunlight reflecting off the snow, according to his advisers, and although his sight is fine, his eyes are sensitive to light.

Jaruzelski does not drink alcoholic beverages or smoke, which is unusual in Poland, where cafés are often hazy with cigarette smoke and special occasions are usually celebrated with a bottle or two of vodka. According to his advisers, Jaruzelski has simple tastes in food and has little interest in sampling local delicacies when he travels abroad on official visits. As a rule, he starts each day with a breakfast consisting of honey and a bit of farmer's cheese on a slice of brown bread along with a cup of tea.

Jaruzelski is reputedly diligent and tireless in carrying out the duties of his office. He has been known to work until two o'clock in the morning and call a staff meeting at six o'clock. Even on such occasions, he is freshly shaven and looking well rested. He reads everything that crosses his desk and meticulously revises his speeches. Occasionally he finds time to put his work aside and go riding at a military stable outside of Warsaw. He has ridden horses all

> *We never treated it as an ideal solution. It is not always possible to choose between good and evil, having to choose instead between the greater and lesser evil. It was the lesser evil.*
> —WOJCIECH JARUZELSKI
> on declaring martial law

Questioned about his decision to impose martial law in Poland and specifically whether he made the decision under the threat of Soviet intervention, Jaruzelski has repeatedly asserted that he does not regret the decision and that the move was necessary to restore order to his country.

his life, and riding remains one of his favorite pastimes.

Jaruzelski's life has not followed a predictable course. He was the son of a wealthy landowner, and he received a religious education, yet he became the leader of a political party that preaches atheism and claims to represent the interests of the working class. The irony of his career is due in no small part to World War II, after which a completely new economic and political system was imposed on Poland by the Soviet Union, which took control of Eastern Europe. Communism seemed to be the wave of the future, at least of Jaruzelski's future. During his lifetime, Jaruzelski has seen Poland go through tumultuous change; he has lived Poland's volatile history. In more recent years, as Poland's leader, he has orchestrated the events that have fundamentally changed Poland, and he will forever be remembered both for the ignominy of imposing martial law and the boldness of moving Poland from totalitarianism toward a more democratic form of government.

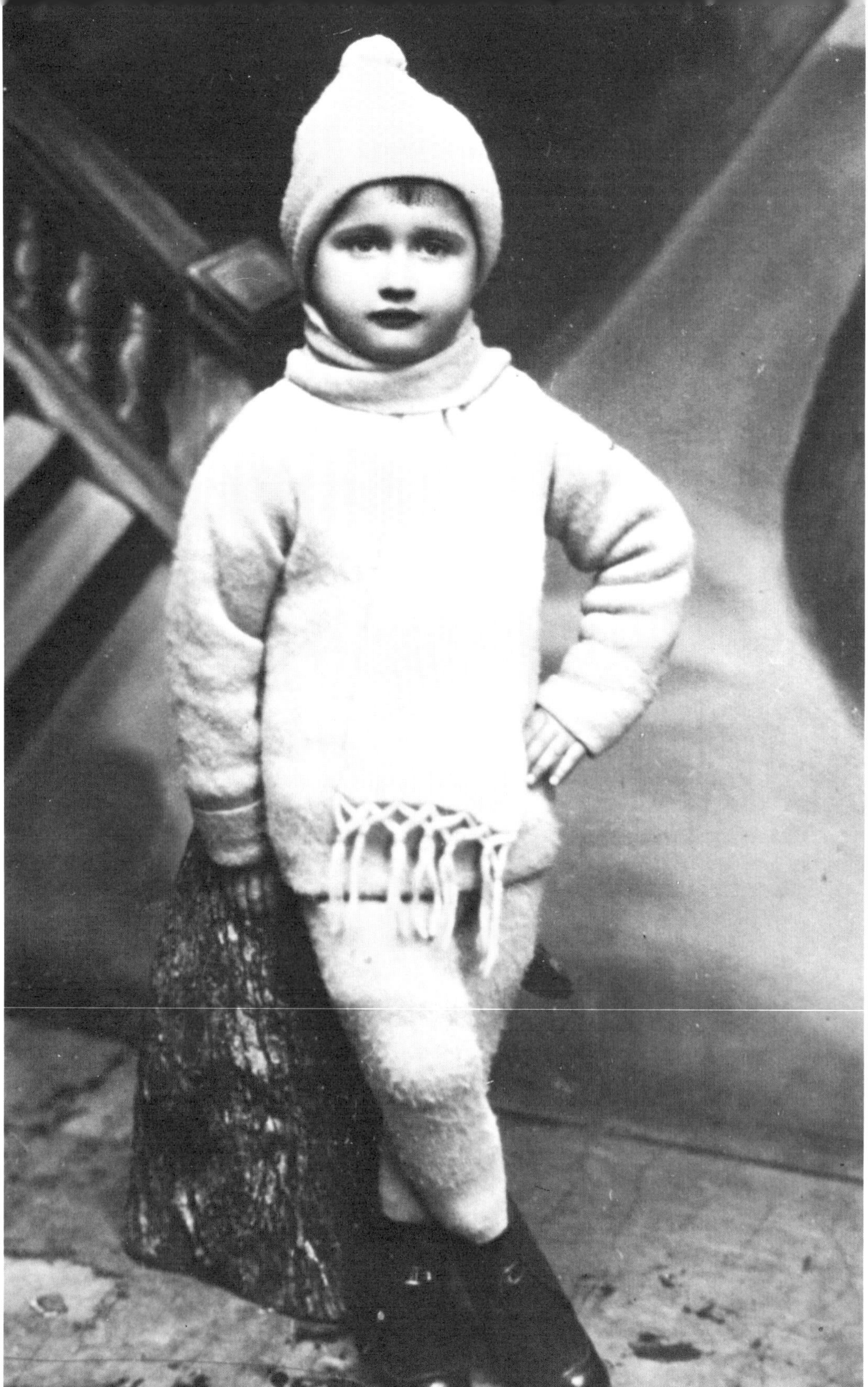

2
A Polish Patriot

Wojciech Jaruzelski was born July 6, 1923. He lived with his parents and younger sister, Teresa, on a family estate in Kurow, near the city of Lublin, about 100 miles southeast of Warsaw. The Jaruzelski family was proud of its long patriotic tradition, and Wojciech, or Wojtek as he was called as a child, was raised on the legends of Polish patriots. He was told stories about the heroic Polish uprisings against foreign oppressors, and he read about the military battles in which his great-grandfather, grandfather, and father had fought as commanding officers. To defend "God, honor, and the fatherland" was the patriotic duty of a Polish nobleman, and generations of Jaruzelskis had all proudly done their part for their country.

From 1795 to 1918, no country named Poland existed. Poland had lost its independence in the late 18th century, when Russia, Prussia, and Austria divided the country into three partitions, one for each of them, and incorporated all Polish lands into their own empires. Poland's powerful neighbors even signed a treaty promising that no territory

> *For two hundred years now, every generation of Poles has had the commandment to save the fatherland encoded in its genes.*
> —TADEUSZ KONWICKI
> Polish novelist

Jaruzelski was born near Lublin, Poland, into a family with a long tradition of military service. Though he emulated his father, grandfather, and great-grandfather, all career military men, Jaruzelski was greatly influenced by his mother, whom he remembers as a person of "great sensitivity and goodness."

Lublin, Poland, located on the Bystrzyca River, approximately 100 miles southeast of Warsaw, was for centuries a major European commercial center. Today it is an important industrial center and the home of five universities.

would ever again be named Poland and literally wiped the country off the map of Europe. When Jaruzelski's great-grandfather, grandfather, and even his father were growing up, Warsaw and Lublin were cities in the Russian Empire. Gdansk (Danzig) and Poznan (Posen) were centers of trade in Prussia, while Kraków and Lvov were part of the Austro-Hungarian Empire. The millions of people who still considered themselves Poles had no country of their own. They were Poles, but they were ruled by the Russian czar, the German kaiser, or the Austrian emperor.

The oppression of Poles was most severe in the Russian partition, where the Jaruzelski family lived. Poles there were expected to give up their Polish culture, to speak Russian, and to pay homage to the Russian czar. Poles were also heavily discriminated against in the Prussian partition, where a policy of Germanization was increasingly forced upon the Slavic residents. All Polish cities and towns were renamed in German. Poles living in the Austrian partition had the greatest degree of autonomy.

There were several desperate attempts to free Poland from Russian oppression. Wojciech's great-grandfather, Władysław Jaruzelski, fought in an uprising against the Russians in 1831, and his grandfather, Wojciech, for whom he was named, commanded a military unit in the January Uprising of 1863. Both efforts were unsuccessful.

Though all men who fought for their country were looked up to for their patriotism and courage, Jaruzelski explains that his grandfather was especially revered. "I was raised in a family and in a circle of society with deep patriotic traditions," he said in 1988. "The story of my grandfather's life, a legend in itself, was of course part of these traditions. I found out about it as a very young boy. . . . I never knew my grandfather personally, because he died before I was born, but his memory was highly cultivated in our family."

General Jaruzelski's grandfather, who was only a teenager when he fought against the Russians, was arrested and sent to Siberia. He was among thousands of Poles, mostly of noble origin, who were deported in 1865 for taking part in the insurrection. As further punishment, the czarist authorities confiscated the Jaruzelski family estate. Even though his grandfather lost the family land, he was greatly admired because he had fought for his country. He returned to Poland from Siberia many years later and married. His wife bore a son, Władysław, in 1895.

When he came of age, Władysław went to study agricultural engineering in Tabor, Czechoslovakia, which was then part of the Austro-Hungarian Empire. While Władysław was at school, England, France, and the United States defeated Germany and Austria in World War I, and Poland became an independent state. Russia, which had been fighting on the side of the victors, dropped out of the war after the Russian Revolution in 1917. The revolution, led by Vladimir Lenin, brought the Bolsheviks into power and gave birth to the Soviet state. With the war over, Władysław returned to Poland in 1918 and became the manager of several farms for a wealthy landowner in the Lublin region.

Poland was an independent country for the first time in almost 125 years, and the Poles reveled in their new independence. Marshal Józef Piłsudski took control of the new republic. For the next three years he went to war against Poland's neighbors to win control of disputed territories and make his reborn nation as big as possible. Władysław Jaruzelski joined the fight as the commander of a cavalry unit.

The Polish army marched eastward in 1919 to gain control over land that had once been part of Poland. Meanwhile, seeking to spread the revolution and extend Soviet power, the Red Army moved west. At first the Poles held the upper hand, claiming territories in Lithuania, Belorussia, and the Ukraine, but in the summer of 1920 the Soviets launched a major offensive and quickly pushed Piłsudski's troops back to the gates of Warsaw. Their long-awaited and newly won independence threatened, the Poles gathered reinforcements and dealt the Soviets an unexpected and shattering defeat.

After being imprisoned by the Russians in 1900 for publishing an underground socialist newspaper and again by the Germans during World War I, Marshal Józef Piłsudski became Polish chief of state in 1918. He later served two terms as Poland's prime minister.

Polish Silesian militiamen go off to battle the Germans in 1921. After World War I and the the Treaty of Versailles in 1919, a bitter territorial dispute arose over Silesia, in central Europe. Poland and Germany both laid claim to the region and clashed repeatedly. The dispute was not settled entirely until after World War II.

Władysław Jaruzelski fought in the Polish-Soviet War of 1919–20, which ended in victory when Polish forces defeated invading Soviet troops and pushed them back to Russian territory. The Treaty of Riga in 1921 gave Poland the contested eastern border lands.

Although at the time most Poles viewed the war as a great patriotic victory, General Jaruzelski views that period of Polish history and the war his father, Władysław, fought in, somewhat differently.

"I see that war as a great unnecessary tragedy. . . . It never elicited the romantic emotions or discussions as did, for example, my grandfather's participation in the January Uprising. It was simply another type of war. The other had its romanticism as an uprising. In general we, Poles, are burdened with the romanticism of uprisings. This has not, after all, always served us well."

As the leader of Communist Poland, Jaruzelski could not say otherwise. After all, Poland had attacked the new Soviet state, whose ideology and leadership Jaruzelski now accepts. The uprisings of the 19th century, on the other hand, can still be glorified; they were against the autocratic czarist government, which was later overthrown by the Russian Revolution itself.

After the war, Władysław Jaruzelski went back to managing farms for the wealthy landowner in Kurów. In 1921 he married the landed nobleman's daughter, Wanda Zaremba, and two years later their son Wojciech, the future leader of Poland, was born.

General Jaruzelski said he was most influenced as a child by his mother, whom he described as "a person of great culture, great sensitivity, and goodness." She taught him poetry and songs. As a young boy Jaruzelski learned a poem that was taught, and continues to be taught, to every Polish child. Written by Władysław Belza, the poem begins with these four lines:

> Kto ty jesteś?
>   Polak maly.
>   Jaki znak twoj?
>   Orzel bialy.

The poem, which has several versions, is in the form of a mother quizzing her young son. In Polish the verses have a simple structure, with every other line rhyming. Here is an English translation:

> Who are you?
> A young Pole.
> What is your sign?
> The white eagle.
> Where do you live?
> Among my own people.
> In what country?
> In the Polish land.
> What is that land?
> My homeland.
> How was it won?
> With blood and scars.
> Do you love her?
> I truly love her.
> What do you believe in?
> I believe in God.*
> What are you to her?
> A thankful child.
> What do you owe her?
> To give up my life.

---

*In postwar versions *God* was changed to *Poland*.

This extremely nationalistic verse can only be appreciated in light of Poland's history. For more than

In 1920, members of the Polish resistance run an underground printing operation during the Polish-Soviet War. Poland's victory in the war led to the signing of the Treaty of Riga in 1921.

100 years, without a country of their own, Poles had struggled to preserve their culture and national identity. Children were taught to love and fight for Poland, even if it meant giving their lives.

Jaruzelski, like all boys, had heroes when he was young. His fictional heroes were from Polish poetry and prose of the early 19th century, the height of Romanticism. His favorite real-life heroes were Prince Józef Poniatowski and Romuald Traugutt. Both were killed during the time of the partitions after taking up arms against the Russians.

Poniatowski, nephew of the last Polish king, joined forces with Napoleon in hopes that a French victory would restore Poland's independence, but when Napoleon's campaign of 1812 against Russia failed and the Grande Armée was driven from Moscow back through Poland and into Germany, Poniatowski and his Polish troops were doomed. At the Battle of the Nations near Leipzig on October 19, 1813, the Polish troops were trapped in the bend of a river by Russian and Prussian forces, a hopeless position symbolic of Poland's historic fate. Poniatowski was wounded and surrounded by enemy sol-

Poles pose in traditional native dress. For centuries, Poles have struggled to preserve not only their independence but also their cultural identity, which has been threatened repeatedly by their large and powerful neighbors.

diers, but he was unwilling to surrender. Heroic death was a more honorable alternative. The prince spurred his horse through the enemy gunfire into the river. "God entrusted me with the honor of the Poles and I shall give it back only to God," were his final words.

Traugutt, another of Jaruzelski's boyhood heroes, was the last leader of the January Uprising of 1863, the insurrection that had made Jaruzelski's grandfather a family hero. Traugutt was caught by the Russians in 1864 and hanged.

Jaruzelski talked about his childhood heroes in an interview with Yugoslavian journalist Zrnka Novak in 1987. He said even though they were anachronistic for 20th-century Europe, their patriotism set good examples for Poles of his generation when World War II broke out in 1939.

"These role models, of course, committed the sin of being one-sided. With their noble and chivalrous ideals, they were an anachronism, but at the same time they contained many intense patriotic impulses and conveyed a sense of honor and duty that

Prince Józef Poniatowski, idolized by the young Jaruzelski, showed such remarkable valor in battle against the Russians that he became a Polish national hero. Rather than surrender to the Russians at Leipzig in 1813, Poniatowski deliberately rode into enemy fire and was killed.

Polish schoolchildren review their lessons. Jaruzelski was given the best education available, receiving instruction from private tutors as a boy and later attending an exclusive secondary school in Warsaw.

allowed my generation to act appropriately in the difficult war effort. And even today they are not without meaning."

Jaruzelski was raised to be a Polish patriot. From an early age he was taught Polish history and literature, which are full of romantic accounts of men who fought for Poland. He learned to ride and fence, necessary skills for young gentlemen at the time. The sons of peasants used horses only for plowing the fields and carting their produce to market, but young noblemen were expected to lead their countrymen into battle to defend Poland, and in those days officers rode on horseback.

Jaruzelski was growing up at a special time in Polish history. Poland was an independent country for the first time in more than 100 years, and the new freedom brought forth an explosion of creative and scholarly activity. Filled with enthusiasm and no longer suppressed by foreign rulers, Polish artists and intellectuals achieved their potential. Experimentation and new discoveries moved Polish mathematicians, economists, and linguists into the forefront of world scholarship, while Polish writers and painters took their place in the European cultural scene.

Poles look back on the interwar period — the 20 years between the end of World War I and the beginning of World War II — with great nostalgia. Yet, Jaruzelski says that during those 20 years life in Poland was backward compared to other European countries. Many people lived in rural villages with no running water or electricity just as their ancestors had lived generations before them. Poland had been ravaged by World War I, not only by the battles that had been played out across its land but also by the pillaging of the German and Russian armies as they retreated through the country. The Germans had even hauled off factory equipment, completely destroying some Polish industries. Poland struggled to get the economy back on its feet and had some success, but by the early 1930s the Great Depression had swept across the United States and Europe. Unemployment was high in Warsaw and other cities, and many of the working-class districts were turning into slums.

In comparison to most Poles during that time, the Jaruzelskis were very well off economically, belonging to a privileged class of noble landowners. Around the time Jaruzelski was born, about 75 percent of Poles lived in the countryside, but the land was owned by only 1 percent of the population. The landowners lived in large manor houses and were entitled to reap the profits of the peasant laborers. Thus, as a young child, Jaruzelski led a comfortable and secure life on his family's country estate. Then it was time to leave home and venture out on his own.

Workers perform their jobs in a thriving Polish textile mill. Poland's industry was ravaged by the Germans during World War I and later by the economic depression of the 1930s. During these years much of Poland was in squalor, but the Jaruzelskis enjoyed the privileges of the noble class of landowners to which they belonged.

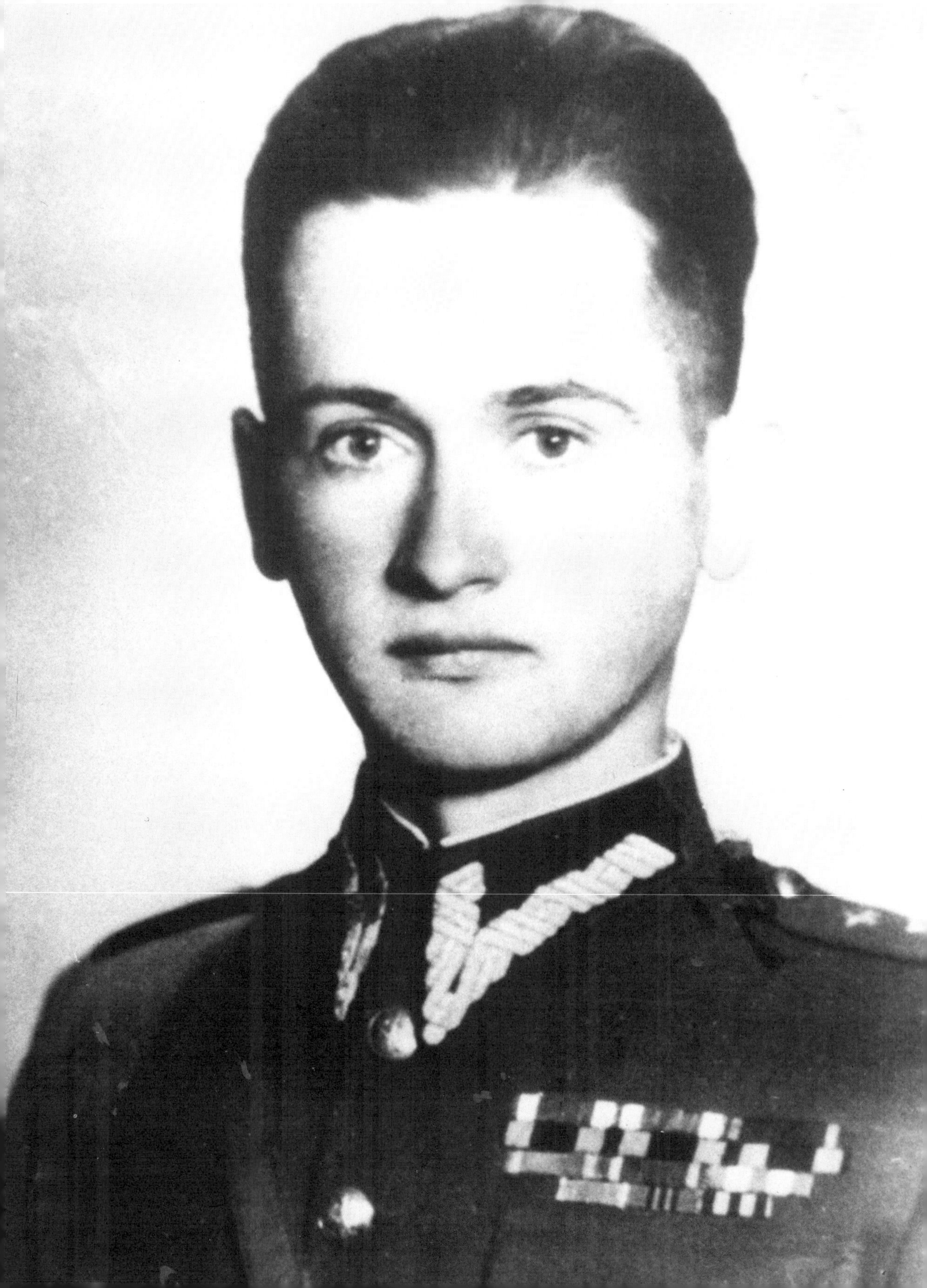

3
A Boy in History

Like most young boys from prosperous families, Wojciech Jaruzelski was educated at home by a private tutor until he reached the age of 10, at which time his parents sent him to a prestigious secondary school in Warsaw. The school was run by Marianist priests. Jaruzelski's parents were practicing Catholics and wanted their young son to continue his studies in a religious atmosphere, but more than that, they wanted him to receive an excellent education, and the best schools at the time were run by priests. Leaving home was an emotional experience for the young Jaruzelski. In 1988 he recalled what it felt like to leave the comforts of family behind.

"When I was ten years old I left home and began my studies at the high school here in Warsaw. It was a traumatic time in my life: My first exam, the first test of my strength. . . . I came from a remote province, from a village, although I was from an educated family, and here I suddenly had to cope with the demands of a new environment and new responsibilities. I stood the test, but I remember

> *I can still remember that sunny September day, the whizzing sounds of German planes strafing against defenseless refugees, exploding bombs, the stench of burning and dead horses at the roadside. I thought the heavens had fallen on me.*
> —WOJCIECH JARUZELSKI
> on the outbreak of World War II

After spending two years in a Nazi labor camp, Jaruzelski joined the Soviet-Polish army in 1943 in hopes of fighting the Germans and defending his homeland. Thus, he carried on the family tradition of military service his great-grandfather had begun.

The Warsaw skyline, 1926. The seat of the Polish government, Warsaw was reduced to rubble by the Germans during World War II. Since its postwar reconstruction, Warsaw has struggled to regain its prominence as an important industrial and cultural center.

how emotional it all was, as was saying good-bye to my mother. That was rough because I was left alone in completely unfamiliar surroundings. I went to a school run by priests — it was owned by priests — and at that time I did not know any of my classmates."

Jaruzelski found the rules and rigors of a Catholic boarding school much different from his quiet, easy life in the country. He had to study hard and attend prayer services every morning and evening. Fifty years later he still remembered how difficult the mathematics lessons were and how he used to dread math tests. He excelled in Polish language and literature, and history soon became his favorite subject. Jaruzelski said that because of his interest in the humanities, he seemed destined to become either an academic or a publicist.

Some of his best memories of those years were of field trips. He and his classmates once sailed down the Vistula River to Kazimierz and Sandomierz, historic Polish cities. Jaruzelski also remembered an excursion to Gniezno, which in the 10th century became the first capital of Poland. Some of his most unpleasant memories from his six years at the school were of when he was sick, and particularly of when he was hospitalized with scarlet fever.

"I was a normal healthy boy, but I had all those childhood diseases which are nearly eliminated today but at that time were quite common — chicken pox, scarlet fever and measles. Scarlet fever was the most serious of them all, and I remember it the most because, since it is a highly contagious disease, I was not able to stay at school. There was an infirmary at the school, where the facilities were very good. Scarlet fever, however, because it is a contagious disease, had to be treated in a special hospital and quarantined. There was, and perhaps still is, such a hospital in Wola, a workers' district in Warsaw. . . . I remember that hospital with such horror . . . frightful, unpleasant conditions."

Jaruzelski was unable to finish school. In 1939, when he was 16 years old, World War II broke out, and he fled with his family to Lithuania. The war, which began in Europe with the German attack on Poland, had been steadily approaching. Germany, under the leadership of Adolf Hitler, annexed Austria in March 1938 and Czechoslovakia in March 1939. Austria had offered little resistance, while Czechoslovakia had been sacrificed by the French and British in an attempt to appease Hitler and prevent the outbreak of war. After Austria and Czechoslovakia were incorporated into the German Reich, Hitler turned his attention to Poland.

Hitler demanded access to Danzig, which at the time did not belong to either Germany or Poland. The Baltic port, claimed by both countries, had been made a free city by the Treaty of Versailles at the end of World War I. The treaty also gave Poland a strip of land leading north to Danzig, the city the Poles called Gdansk. While giving Poland access to the Baltic Sea, the so-called Polish Corridor cut

The Italian dictator Benito Mussolini (left), German chancellor Adolf Hitler (second from left), and British prime minister Neville Chamberlain (right) meet with the aid of an interpreter in Munich, Germany, in 1938. A year later, the Germans invaded Poland, beginning World War II.

through German lands, separating East Prussia from West Prussia. Although Hitler limited his demands to Danzig and the Polish Corridor, it was clear that he ultimately wanted much more.

Despite the danger Hitler's Germany presented, Poles would not consider forming an alliance with the Soviet Union. They did not want Soviet troops to set foot on Polish soil, fearing that once the Soviets were in Poland, they would never leave. Instead, Poles put their faith in the French and the British, who indeed had seemed to realize that giving in to Hitler's demands had done nothing to lessen the threat of war. British prime minister Neville Chamberlain announced on March 31, 1939, in the House of Commons, that if Hitler attacked, Britain would come to Poland's defense: "In the event of any action which clearly threatened Polish independence and which the Polish government accordingly considered it vital to resist with their na-

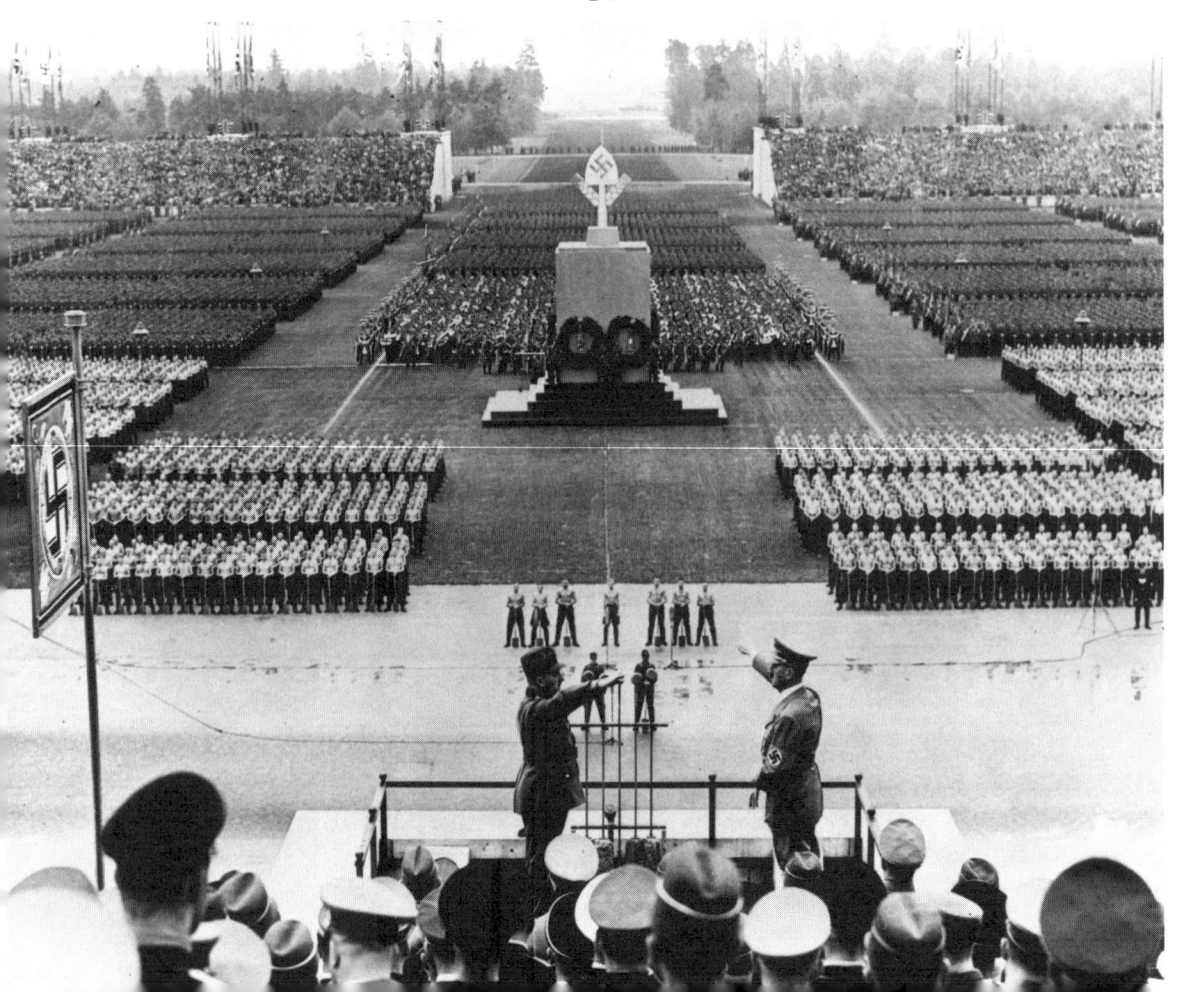

Hitler (with swastika arm band) salutes a German labor leader at a Nazi rally in Nuremberg, Germany, in 1938. Germany's desperate need for leadership and his extraordinary charisma combined to place Hitler in a position of power from which he could direct and inspire the Nazi war machine.

tional forces, His Majesty's Government would feel themselves bound at once to lend the Polish government all support in their power." The French government joined in the British guarantee.

Hitler pressed on and shocked the allies by making an agreement with Soviet leader Joseph Stalin. With the Nazi-Soviet Non-Aggression Pact, signed August 23, 1939, Germany and the Soviet Union vowed never to attack each other. The pact also contained a secret protocol that made provisions for the partition of Poland and the Baltic countries, setting the scene for a joint attack on Poland and the division of Polish territory between Germany and the Soviet Union. As in past centuries, Poland was once again carved up by its powerful neighbors.

Hitler's forces attacked Poland on September 1, 1939. The fighting broke out before dawn, when the German battleship *Schleswig-Holstein*, in Danzig on a "friendship visit," opened fire on the Polish fort at Westerplatte. Within hours the tanks of the German blitzkrieg (lightning war) were racing across Poland's borders. The Luftwaffe bombed Polish airfields, destroying nearly all the Polish aircraft before they could get off the ground, and then began bombing Polish cities.

Britain and France declared war on Germany on September 3, 1939, two days after the attack on Poland. World War II had officially begun. Yet, despite their guarantees, neither of the Western allies would fire a single shot to help the Poles, who fought bravely but were overwhelmed by Hitler's military machine. By the end of the second week of fighting, the Nazi forces had surrounded Warsaw, but the Poles did not give up. On September 17, 1939, the Soviet army marched into Poland from the east to claim its share of the besieged country. Attacked from both sides, and receiving no assistance from its allies, the Poles defended their capital city until September 28, when the Germans and Soviets signed a treaty to finalize the division of Poland. The demarcation line was set along the Bug and San rivers, which put Warsaw and Lublin under German control. Poles would suffer the terror of occupation for the next six years.

Poles scramble for shelter as the German Luftwaffe bombs Warsaw in September 1939. To escape the Nazi onslaught, the 16-year-old Jaruzelski fled with his family to Lithuania.

Hitler, his arm outstretched in a Nazi salute, reviews a squadron of tanks in Warsaw on October 5, 1939. When the Germans and the Soviets divided Polish territory between them in September of that year, Warsaw and Lublin remained in German hands.

At the time, the Poles were not given much credit for their military efforts to defend their homeland. The Polish army's collapse after only 35 days appeared to be a humiliating defeat, but this was before the world had realized what a powerful weapon of war the Nazis had created. The Western allies were soon to have their turn against the forces of the German Wehrmacht, and they would fare no better than the Poles did. The Germans launched their attack on the Western front on May 10, 1940, and quickly moved through the Netherlands, Belgium, and into France. After 5 days the Dutch army capitulated; after 17 days a defeated British Expeditionary Force, forced to retreat back across the English Channel, started the evacuation of about 338,000 men from Dunkirk, France; and after 18 days the Belgian army surrendered. On the 34th day the Germans occupied Paris, and three days later the new French government, under Marshal Philippe Pétain, asked the Germans for an armistice. Unwilling to have their capital reduced to rubble as Warsaw had been, the French gave up Paris without a fight.

The plight of the Jews in German-occupied Poland is well known. Herded first into walled city ghettos, they were later transported to extermination camps. About 3 million Polish Jews, as well as millions more from other parts of Europe, were killed by the Nazis. Non-Jewish Poles were murdered as well. Some of the first mass killings in German-occupied Poland were of Polish intellectuals. Professors, teachers, writers, and priests were herded into camps, where thousands were shot. As the Nazis took over the country, they forced many Poles from their homes and often killed the active or prominent members of communities. By getting rid of those Poles who could lead or influence others, the Germans hoped to make the task of controlling the hostile inhabitants of Poland a little easier. It was fear of such Nazi treatment that caused the Jaruzelski family to flee to Lithuania.

Soon after claiming portions of Poland, the Soviets moved to take control of the Baltic states as provided for in the nonaggression pact. The Soviet

Union signed so-called mutual-assistance pacts with Lithuania, Latvia, and Estonia, and then sent in troops to occupy these countries. The Baltic states were later annexed into the Soviet Union. This was precisely the fate Poles had feared when a similar treaty between Poland and the Soviet Union was discussed in 1939 before the German attack.

The Soviet NKVD, or secret police, treated Poles in the Soviet-occupied territories no better than they were treated by the Gestapo in areas under German control. A decree issued in Wilno, the capital of Lithuania, listed the categories of people who would be deported to labor camps in Siberia. Included on the long list were men who had fought against the Red Army in the period 1918–21 as well as aristocrats and landowners. Also on the list were officers and soldiers who were currently in any army other than the Soviet army, people who had traveled abroad, the staff of the Red Cross, priests, wealthy merchants, bankers, owners of hotels and restaurants, and even stamp collectors. Anyone with any prominence or who had contact with people in other countries was considered a threat to the Soviet

Having failed to stop the German advance on the western front, the British Expeditionary Force makes a hasty retreat across the English Channel in May 1940.

During the German occupation of Poland, Polish Jews were forced to wear arm bands for identification. Then, they were systematically taken from their homes and placed in ghettos such as this one before being transported to so-called work camps, where they were put to death. Some 3 million Polish Jews were killed by the Nazis.

Union. Jaruzelski's father was clearly targeted, and his family was deported in 1940 to a labor camp in Bijsk, a small city in the Altai Mountains, not far from the Mongolian border.

In an article published in November 1987 in the Soviet journal *Kommunist*, Jaruzelski wrote that the deportations were "contrary to Poland's right to independence." His statement was evidence of a new policy that has put an end to decades of official silence about the deportations and other Soviet actions during the war. In April 1987, Jaruzelski and Soviet leader Mikhail Gorbachev set up a joint commission to review the history of Polish-Soviet relations, and in the spirit of Gorbachev's policy of *glasnost*, or openness, the communist leaders agreed that there should no longer be any "blank spots" in their countries' mutual history. Also, the existence of the secret protocol of the Nazi-Soviet pact and the true nature of the Soviet invasion in 1939 were acknowledged for the first time.

Another episode that came under review was the massacre of Polish officers in the Katyn Forest during World War II. The Soviets blamed the murders on the Nazis, but for most historians Soviet guilt has been established beyond a reasonable doubt. The bodies of 4,000 Polish officers were discovered in a mass grave in the Katyn Forest, near the Soviet city of Smolensk, in April 1943. Most of the officers had their hands tied behind their backs and each had a bullet in the back of his head. The dead were among the 15,000 officers who had been captured when the Soviet Union invaded Poland in September 1939. The bodies of the remaining 11,000 were never found. For Poles, the Katyn massacre is one of the greatest unpunished crimes of the war years and a symbol of the Soviet Union's heinous treatment of Poland.

Members of the Jaruzelski family were among the millions of Poles who suffered at the hands of the Soviets. The teenage Jaruzelski, his parents, and younger sister were driven from their home and deported to a labor camp in a cold, remote region of the Soviet Union. Jaruzelski was put to work in a forest where trees were being cut down for lumber

Near Warsaw, a Polish student suspected of spying is arrested by the German military and sent to prison. During the occupation, the Nazis killed or jailed Polish intellectuals, clergy, and others who they thought might inspire Poles to resist and perhaps rebel against the German forces.

and fuel. In the beginning his job was to carry the fallen logs out of the forest, but later he was given a job chopping down the trees. His food rations depended on the number of trees he cut down, and Jaruzelski, who was doing manual labor for the first time in his life, had to work hard to fulfill the daily norms. Conditions were harsh in the mountainous northern region: Temperatures were well below zero degrees Fahrenheit for much of the year, snow was often several feet deep, and the sunlight reflecting off of it produced a strong glare, making the difficult work even more demanding. Jaruzelski adjusted to these conditions, but his father was not so resilient. Władysław Jaruzelski died in the camp in 1942 at the age of 47.

The next year Wojciech Jaruzelski was able to leave the labor camp to join a Polish army that was formed in the Soviet Union under Soviet command. He would return to Poland as an army officer and fight to drive the Germans back to Berlin. It would be his way of serving his country and continuing the patriotic tradition of his and many other Polish families. Like his father, grandfather, and great-grandfather, he would risk his life to defend Poland. The difference was that he would be fighting with the Russians instead of against them.

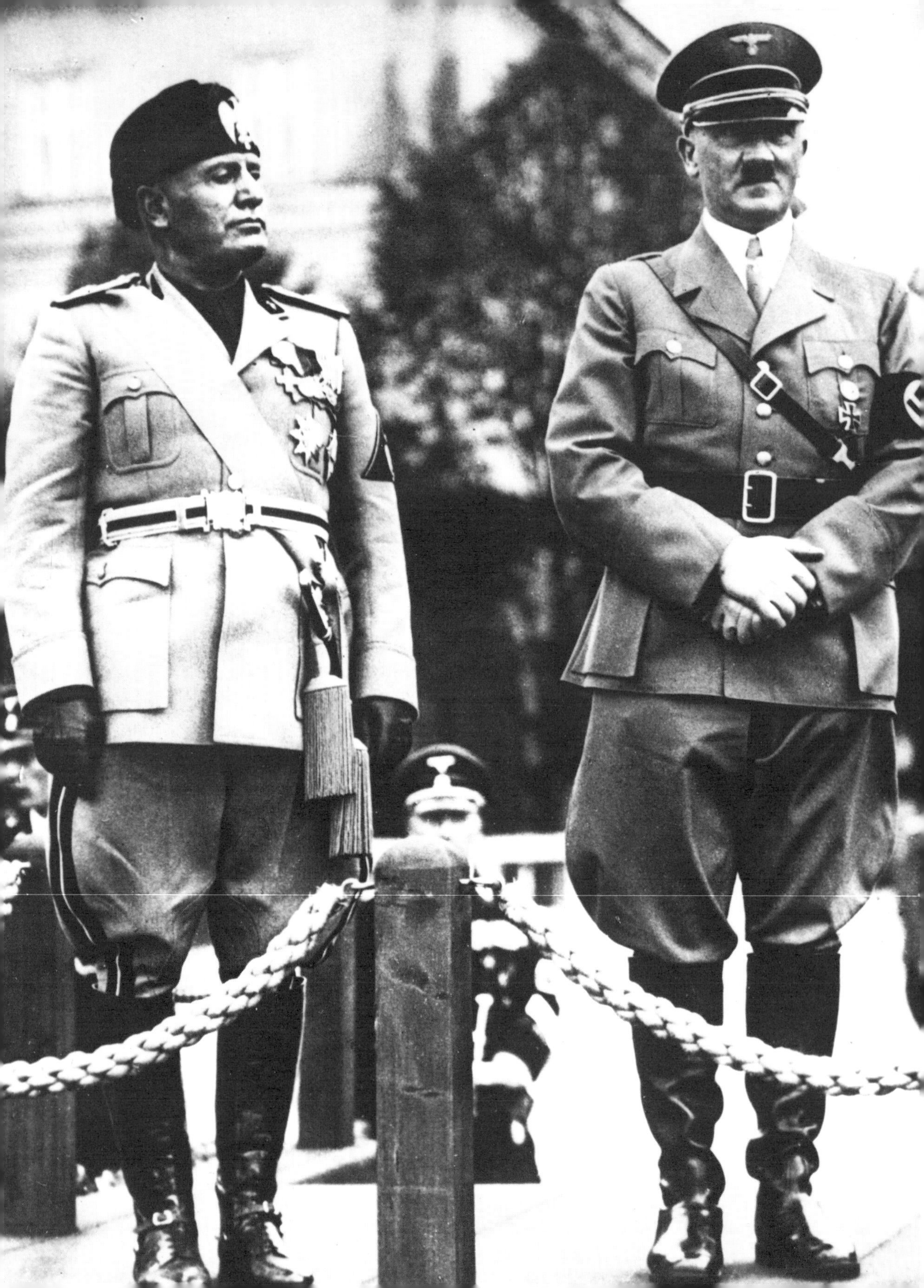

4
The Fascist Menace

Nazi Germany invaded the Soviet Union in June 1941 and put an end to the dubious alliance formed by their nonaggression pact. With Hitler's troops and tanks advancing deep into Russia, Poles in the Soviet Union found themselves in a much better position than before: Stalin needed their help to push the Germans back across Poland to Berlin.

A Polish army was formed under General Władysław Anders, but Stalin did little to help Poles make their way from remote camps to where the troops were stationed. Relations between Anders and Stalin became strained, and the Polish commander refused to join the Soviet campaign, afraid that he and his troops would be taken under Soviet command as the armies moved west. He did not trust the Soviets and did not want them to be the ones to liberate Poland from the Germans. Anders led his troops out of the Soviet Union through Iran in 1942 and later fought under British command in the North African and Italian campaigns.

> *There should be one master only for the Poles, the Germans. Two masters side by side cannot and must not exist. Therefore all representatives of the Polish intelligentsia are to be exterminated.*
> —ADOLF HITLER

The leaders of the Axis powers, Mussolini and Hitler, were charismatic missionaries of hatred and violence. With loud, impassioned speeches and elaborate symbolism, they publicly indulged their own twisted fantasies and intimidated entire nations with fascist military might.

General Zygmunt Berling was Jaruzelski's commander during World War II.

Jaruzelski did not join this army. He joined a second Polish army formed by General Zygmunt Berling, a Polish officer who agreed to serve under Soviet command. The tide of the war had turned at the battle at Stalingrad, and by spring of 1943 the Soviet army was pushing the German army back through hundreds of miles of Soviet territory. Berling, who wanted Poles to fight the Germans on the eastern front, recruited Polish deportees for what became the First Polish Army.

Jaruzelski was sent to the Polish Officers' School in Ryazan, south of Moscow, where he was trained in a heavy-machine-gun company. There he studied the political and economic theories of the German philosopher Karl Marx and the theories of Lenin. In the autumn of 1943, Jaruzelski was given command of a platoon in the Fifth Regiment of the Jan Henryk Dabrowski Second Infantry Division, and a few months later he took command of a regimental field-reconnaissance unit.

Soviet and Polish troops reached the Bug River on July 19, 1944. The Soviets considered the river to be the boundary between Poland and the Soviet Union, although the prewar border had been many miles to the east. Jaruzelski, accepting the Soviet version of the map, was among the first to cross the river into Poland.

"It is not surprising, after all, that my return to a country for which I had longed for six years was an extremely important moment, which is still fresh in my mind and heart," Jaruzelski recalled in 1988. "When we crossed the Bug River, the border at the time, I was the commander of a reconnaissance cavalry platoon, which meant that I led the way, that I was the spearhead of that unit. So I was among the first in my formation to enter Polish territory."

Jaruzelski was also among the troops to march into Lublin, a Polish city near where he had grown up. It was there on July 22 that the Soviets created the Polish Committee of National Liberation (PKWN) and gave it the powers of a temporary government of Poland. The leaders of the new government, known in the west as the Lublin Committee, were Polish Communists who had spent the war years in the Soviet Union.

The Soviet army's advance tolled the death knell for members of the Polish resistance, who during the occupation had been fighting an underground guerrilla war against the Germans in Poland and preparing for the day when they could rise up in force. The Soviets, however, considered these resistance fighters a threat to Soviet military and political control of Poland because of their anti-Communist stance, so they took steps to get rid of them. As Soviet troops moved into Poland, they were followed by Soviet security forces, the forerunners of the KGB. The Soviets replaced all local officials and arrested members of the Polish resistance as they emerged from the underground to fight the retreating Germans.

The largest group within the resistance movement was the Armia Krajowa, or Home Army. The Home Army pledged its allegiance to the Polish government-in-exile in London, which was recognized by the United States and the rest of the Western allies as the legitimate government of Poland. Members of the Home Army who fought alongside the Soviet army to push the Germans out of Wilno and

A Soviet gun crew defends Stalingrad against the Germans in 1943. The surrender of the German Sixth Army at Stalingrad crushed Hitler's hope of victory in the Soviet Union and marked a critical juncture in his ultimate demise.

Lvov, now cities in the Soviet Union, found themselves under Soviet arrest after the battles had been won. In Lublin, Home Army units took control of the city before the Soviet army arrived, but they, too, were arrested. Lublin was handed over to the communist PKWN. This pattern would be repeated many times as the Soviet army swept through Poland.

To Jaruzelski, the Soviets, together with their Polish allies, were liberating Poland. They were the ones driving out the Germans, who had committed untold atrocities during the six years of their occupation. It was outside Lublin that Jaruzelski first saw the horrors of the Nazi death camps.

"I was a witness to the ravages of fascist crime. Located on the outskirts of Lublin was one of the concentration camps—Majdanek. We marched past that camp. I saw the prisoners' barracks, the crematoriums, half-charred bodies. It was a revolting sight, but I was to see much more of such things later on. The last such camp I saw was the Oranienburg-Sachsenhausen camp north of Berlin. One of the things we did there was to liberate the camp."

Majdanek was one of many concentration camps built in Poland by the Nazis. The most notorious one was at Auschwitz, with adjoining facilities at Birkenau. The camps became centers of systematic genocide in 1942, when Hitler instituted his Final Solution, a program designed to kill all the Jews in Europe. About 3 million Polish Jews were killed, or 9 out of every 10 Jews who had been living in Poland when the war broke out, while an additional 3 million Jews from other countries in Europe also died during the Holocaust. All told, the Nazis annihilated two-thirds of the prewar Jewish population in Europe. Along with the Jews, another 9 to 10 million non-Jews died in Nazi concentration camps. Most were Gypsies and Slavs, mainly Poles, Ukrainians, and Belorussians.

Hitler's near annihilation of Polish Jews changed the ethnic composition of Poland, which before the war had the largest Jewish population in Europe. About 10 percent of the population was Jewish, with the figure rising much higher in many cities.

Two dying prisoners at a Nazi concentration camp lie among their dead comrades on a barracks floor. In 1944, the Polish Home Army attempted to liberate Poland from Nazi clutches. The Germans crushed the rebellion, however, killing 200,000 Poles, while the Soviets did nothing.

About 40 percent of the people living in Warsaw when Jaruzelski was there as a young student were Jewish. Today less than 5,000 practicing Jews live in Poland.

Meanwhile, Soviet and Polish troops were continuing to march west through Poland in 1943 and 1944. The Soviets' unwillingness to join forces with the Home Army and their treatment of the Polish resistance fighters placed the Home Army in a difficult situation. Poles had longed for a time when they would be able to defeat the Germans and once again govern their own land, but instead they were being forced to watch as the Soviets took control of Poland. The leaders of the Home Army were frustrated. With Soviet troops moving closer and closer to Warsaw, they decided to act and stake a claim on their nation's capital. The plan was to seize Warsaw as the Germans withdrew and before the Soviets had a chance to claim the city for themselves.

The uprising was launched August 1, 1944, and for the next two months the brave but poorly armed resistance fighters struggled against the powerful Nazi military machine. The Germans drove their tanks safely through Warsaw by roping Polish

Polish troops, under the leadership of General Berling, dislodge Germans from Praga, a Warsaw suburb, in 1944. The Poles were turned back, however, and for the time being Warsaw remained in German hands.

Despite the Polish Home Army's valiant effort to defend their homeland, German air raids reduced Warsaw to ashes and rubble in 1944. When the Soviets finally joined Poland to fight the Nazis, they did so as part of a plan to conquer Poland, not to set it free.

women and children to the sides. They sent war planes over the city to drop bombs on apartment buildings and hospitals. The Home Army, which had neither tanks nor planes, was forced out of Warsaw, section after section. The Germans shot thousands of the remaining residents in mass executions.

Some hope came in the middle of September, when General Berling's Polish troops took Praga, a district separated from the rest of Warsaw by the Vistula River. But Berling's army suffered heavy casualties when it tried to cross the river, and after one briefly successful crossing it was forced to withdraw. Jaruzelski was close enough to watch Warsaw's destruction, but he was powerless to do anything about it. Soviet troops made no effort to help the embattled Poles in Warsaw.

The Home Army surrendered on October 2, 1944. The Polish resistance fighters were taken prisoner by the Germans, who then deported the entire population of Warsaw to concentration camps or to forced labor in Germany. Warsaw was empty, the uprising was crushed, but still the Germans were not satisfied. Hitler ordered that Warsaw be "razed without a trace," and demolition squads began systematically blowing up the city, reducing its houses, shops, churches, and palaces to piles of ashes and stone. When the Soviet army, together with its Polish troops, finally advanced into Warsaw on January 17, 1945, more than 90 percent of the buildings had been destroyed or damaged beyond repair. Jaruzelski, now a lieutenant and commander of a reconnaissance unit, was among the first Polish soldiers to march into what was left of Warsaw.

"Warsaw was the most shocking sight of all," he recalled. "For me the impact was doubled. Warsaw, the capital, is a symbol for me as for all Poles. Warsaw was also a part of my youth. For six years I lived here and studied here. . . . As it happened, on January 17, . . . we entered from the north — Zolibórz, Powazki. It was a horrifying sight. It was a desert, a stone desert. And it was cold. It was dusted with snow. It was impossible to get through some streets because they were blocked by rubble."

Berling's army continued the march west, his Polish troops helping the Soviets break through German defenses on the Pommernstellung, or Pomeranian Wall, in northern Poland and drive the Germans out of Poland. As a reconnaissance officer, Jaruzelski's mission was to go ahead of the rest of the army and learn the position of enemy troops. He made his way through the woods and fields on horseback. In the course of about a year, Jaruzelski rode from Belorussia to the Elbe River (now the border between Poland and Germany) and then back to central Poland.

Jaruzelski was wounded twice during the campaign, but never seriously enough to take him out of action for long. The first time he caught a bullet in his thigh, but after three days in the hospital he was back in the front ranks. A couple of weeks later, while he was fighting on the Pomeranian Wall, a piece of shrapnel grazed his forehead. Unlike so many of his compatriots, he lived to see the end of the war in Europe. On May 4, as Jaruzelski and the

In 1945, the Soviet leader Joseph Stalin issued this commendation to Jaruzelski for his bravery in the service of his country. As a reconnaissance officer fighting the Germans, Jaruzelski was wounded twice during the Pomeranian Wall campaign in northern Poland.

Polish troops neared the Elbe River, they saw a strange flag flying on the other side. It was red, white, and blue.

"We fought in Pomerania and along the Baltic Sea, we forced the Oder River and finally reached the Elbe, where, indeed, we made contact with American soldiers. They were an exoticism, for we knew about Americans only from films, and at that time even in that way not very well. Those first contacts were friendly, very friendly. Everyone was so happy it was all over."

When Germany surrendered in May 1945, Poland was in the hands of Soviet troops. Poland had won the war but not its freedom; one occupying power had been traded for another. Poles had fought alongside French and British troops to defeat the Germans on foreign soil, and in Poland they had waged their own battle against the Nazis. Poles had fought on the side of the victors, but they were not to share in the rewards of victory. They were neglected by the Western powers, while the Soviets treated them more like enemies than allies.

Poland's fate had been discussed at the wartime conferences of the "Big Three": U.S. president Franklin Roosevelt, British prime minister Winston Churchill, and Soviet leader Joseph Stalin. The first meeting was held in Tehran, Iran, at the end of 1943. The Soviets at that time were bearing the main burden of the fight against Germany, so the British and Americans, who had not yet launched an offensive on the Western front, were in no position to argue with the Soviets over Poland. As the Allied leaders formulated their strategy for defeating Germany, they agreed that after the war Europe would be divided into zones of influence, with Poland in the Soviet zone. Even so, President Roosevelt believed Poland would have considerable independence.

The Big Three met again in February 1945 in Yalta, on the Crimean peninsula in the Soviet Union. An end was in sight for the war in Europe, but an Allied victory in the Pacific theater was still in doubt. Churchill and especially Roosevelt were once again more interested in maintaining good relations with Stalin, this time to win his support for the war against Japan, than in arguing about the fate of Poland. The American and British leaders made a token effort to assure Poland's independence by insisting that non-Communist Poles from a London government-in-exile be included in a new Polish government. Yet, even if they had been willing to push harder for an independent Poland, by 1945 it was too late: Almost all of Poland was controlled by the Soviet army.

When Poland emerged from World War II, it was a much different country than it had been before the war. For one thing, it was not in the same place on the map; it had been picked up and moved 150 to 200 miles to the west. Poland lost its Lithuanian, Belorussian, and Ukrainian lands to the Soviet Union and in return was given a band of German territory to the west and north, which included Silesia, Pomerania, and East Prussia. Germans who lived in those areas were transported to Germany, leaving their houses and farms to Polish refugees and families from the east, whose homes now lay inside the Soviet Union.

Meanwhile, Poles who had been deported to labor camps in the Soviet Union or to forced labor in Germany during the war returned home. Jaruzelski's mother and sister returned to Poland in 1946. His mother died in 1966, and his sister, who settled in Łódź, became a scholar of the Polish language.

The emerging government of postwar Poland was subordinate to the Soviet Union. The elections that Stalin had agreed to at the Yalta conference were repeatedly postponed, and when they were finally held in January 1947, they were neither free nor democratic. The candidates were picked by the Soviets or their Polish protégés, who then still felt it necessary to control how people cast their ballots. Workers from entire factories were escorted to the polls and told to vote for the government's candidates or else they would lose their jobs. The Communists claimed 80 percent of the vote and moved to take complete control of the government. During the course of the next year, Poland was transformed into a Soviet-style one-party state.

The "Big Three" (left to right) — British prime minister Winston Churchill, U.S. president Franklin Roosevelt, and Soviet leader Joseph Stalin — meet in February 1945 at Yalta, in the Soviet Union. The issue of Poland's independence, not only from the Germans but also from the Soviets, was on the Yalta agenda.

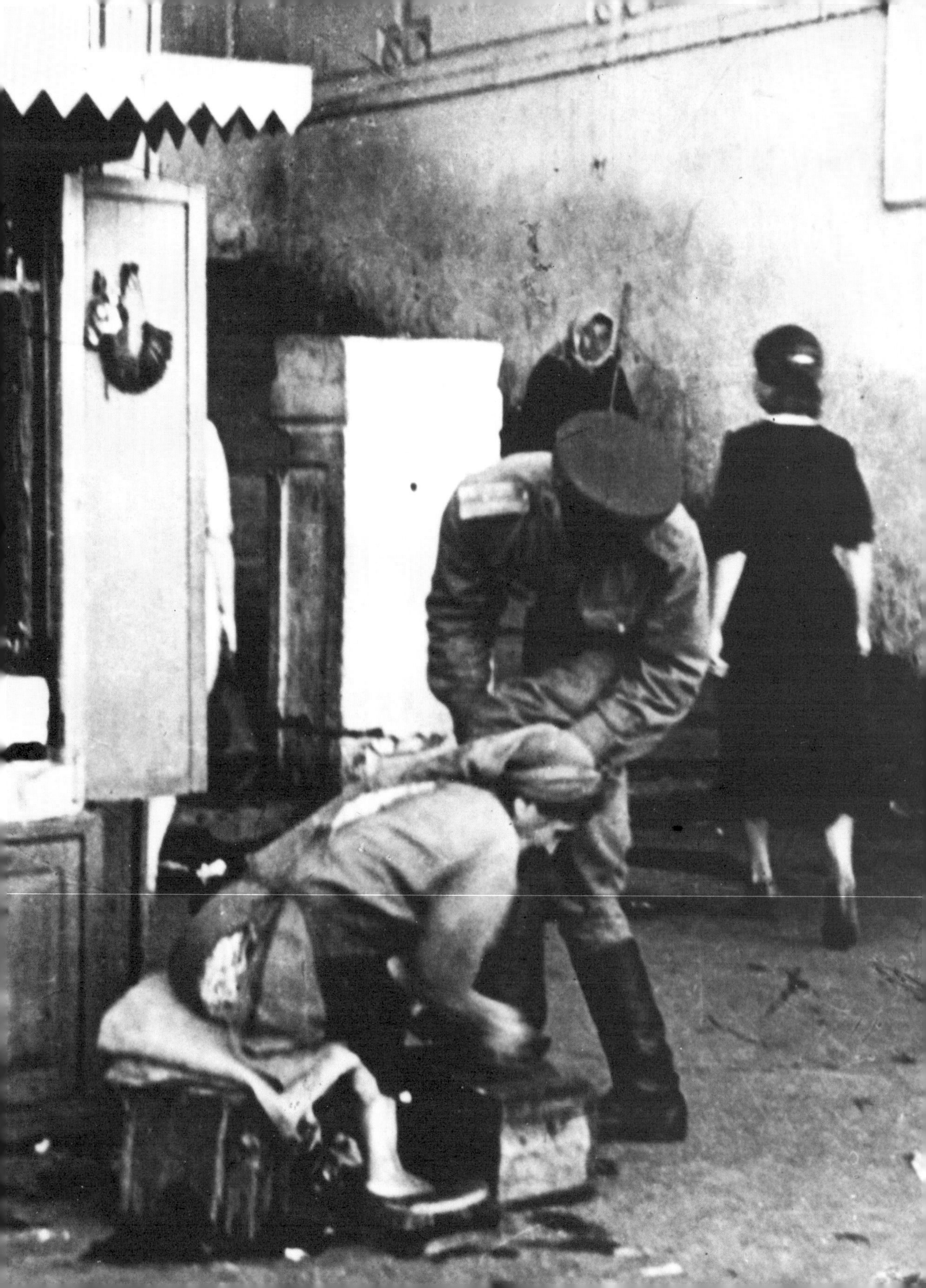

5
The Face of Communism

World War II ended in 1945. The Soviet army had driven the Germans out of Poland and the Communists, backed up by the army, were setting up a new government in Warsaw. For Wojciech Jaruzelski, who was 22 years old in 1945, communism was the wave of the future. He decided to stay in the army for the time being, join the Communist party, and help build a Communist state in Poland on the model of the Soviet Union.

For Jaruzelski the battles continued for another two years. The Soviet army and its Polish troops faced armed resistance from several anti-Communist guerrilla organizations that were trying to prevent the Communist takeover. It was then that Jaruzelski decided he would give up his plans of becoming a historian and make the military his career.

"At the end of the war the battle with the reactionary forces intensified and elements of an outright civil war appeared," Jaruzelski told Yugoslavian journalist Zrnka Novak in 1987. "I took an active part in the war, which in a practical sense lasted until 1947. Leaving the army at that time would have been a type of desertion.

> *In World War II, Poland lost everything except her honor, except her dreams.*
> —GEORGE BUSH
> U.S. president, from an address given at the Solidarity monument in Gdansk, July 11, 1989

A Polish woman stoops to buff the boots of a Soviet military officer during the postwar period. By the end of World War II, the Soviets had replaced the Germans as the occupying force in Poland, and Jaruzelski joined the Communist party.

After World War II, Jaruzelski (left), in his early 20s, decided to pursue a military career and fight to secure a communist future for Poland. The army is "my home, my family, my passion," he said. "The army is a great school."

"At the same time, in the course of those years the army had become my home, my family, my passion. In the army I had a friend. I had made a career for myself and, despite my young age, I already had a lot of experience. Staying in the army was natural; it let me continue a service that I loved and that was in accordance with my convictions and sense of duty. I felt in the army I could complete my education and acquire knowledge in new areas. The army is a great school."

Jaruzelski continued his education in military academies in Poland and the Soviet Union. He entered the Higher Infantry School in Rembertow, outside of Warsaw, in early 1947, and after completing the military school he became a lecturer there in tactics and staff work. He later graduated from the General Staff Academy in Warsaw and completed a course in strategic studies at Moscow's Voroshylov Military Academy. He was promoted to lieutenant colonel in 1949 and to full colonel in 1954.

At the military academies, Jaruzelski once more immersed himself in the study of Marxist ideology, which was as important a part of the curriculum as military strategy. He joined the Communist party in 1947.

"You arrive at Marxism either through books or through life's experiences," Jaruzelski explained in 1988. "I arrived through life's experiences. And that was by far not the simplest way, for my family background, my childhood and my schooling, one might say, led in a quite opposite direction.

"My mother instilled in me a certain type of sensitivity — a moral sensitivity, a sense of justice for other people. . . . Perhaps because of that I was more deeply affected by the impressions, observations, and experiences of those years, when I clearly saw what fascism and reaction really meant, when I confronted my past views of the Soviet Union and of Russians in particular.

"I was brought up to believe that every Russian was an enemy, that every Russian was an evil person. There, when I was living in those very harsh conditions [in Siberia], I saw that a Russian can be a true friend, that he can be a good person. I can honestly say that they are good people. I saw the Russians at their most difficult time, and I was able to match what I had been taught with what I saw when they were experiencing the enormous hardships and burdens imposed by the war."

Remember that Russia had been Poland's enemy for hundreds of years, and only a few years before Jaruzelski was born, Poles had waged a bitter battle against the Soviets to defend their country's newly regained independence. Jaruzelski, like most Poles, was raised to hate the Russians, but when he was deported to Siberia to live and work among them, he found they were not bad people, after all. He said the local Russians were kind to him and shared what little food they had with him and the other Polish deportees. He saw the great sacrifices that the Russians made during the war. More people from the Soviet Union than from any other country, as many as 20 to 25 million, lost their lives during the war. (The percentage, however, was higher in

> *Russia is inextricably woven into the history of Europe—not only as an adversary and danger but also as a partner—historical, political, cultural, and economic.*
> —WILLY BRANDT
> German chancellor

Poland, where 6 million people died, or almost 1 in 5 of the prewar population.) Because Jaruzelski had expected to hate the Russians he would meet in the Soviet Union, he was surprised to find that they were kind and generous, especially toward a Polish teenager far from home.

"Let me put it this way," he said in 1988, "when something clashes with an old stereotype in such a radical way, then the reaction is even stronger. Of course I don't want to glorify that period. It was a very difficult time of my life. Though only a young boy, I was in Siberia working hard. I saw the many injustices of the Stalinist period, although at that time I was not able to comprehend them as I comprehend and see them today.

"But what was important to me then were the people and a certain degree of social justice, in that I saw human poverty but no affluence in the background. I felt that to be most important and characteristic, especially when I compared it with what I remembered from the prewar period in Poland, when I saw the two extremes. Destitution, streets full of beggars with outstretched hands . . . and at the same time, the splendor and enormous riches of the few. All those impressions were stored away."

The "injustices of the Stalinist period" that Jaruzelski referred to have now been condemned in the Soviet Union and the countries of Eastern Europe as well as in the West. Stalin sent millions of his own people to prisons and labor camps because of their political views or because they were associated with a group that the Soviet leader considered a threat to his absolute control. He executed approximately 2 million Soviet citizens, including many Communist party members and most of the top military officers, leaving the army with few experienced commanders when the war broke out. His agricultural policy of forced collectivization produced a horrible famine that was responsible for many more deaths in the 1930s.

The extent of Stalin's crimes was not known during the war and was not revealed until after his death in 1953. What impressed Jaruzelski in the Soviet Union in the early 1940s was a sense of social

If this world of ours is going to be a safe place to live in, it must be a world where equal partnership and diversity are real rather than merely theoretical values.
—WOJCIECH JARUZELSKI

equality, even if it meant that people were equally poor. Jaruzelski said his gradual conversion to Marxism continued when he joined Berling's army.

"Then came the army and contact with many people who were more educated than I was on that score — in other words, Marxists, Polish and Soviet Communists. It was a long process and a long road. Yet I have to emphasize that at that time my conversion to Marxism had nothing to do with Marxist theory, but was still on the level of perceptions and pure human feelings.

"The end of the war was followed by a fight against the reactionary groups, both Ukrainian and Polish, which gave me a better picture of the contradictions that exist in a society. Only then did I have a chance to begin to read, study, and eventually graduate from military academies, working hard to further my education. In that way, personal experience was supplemented by the knowledge and learning that led me to the world outlook that guides me today."

Karl Marx believed that when the factories and industries are privately owned, as they are in capitalist countries, society is divided into two distinct classes of people — the capitalist class and the working class, or proletariat. The workers, Marx said, are not paid the value of their labor, and they do not have control over their working conditions. Rather, they are exploited by the capitalists, who are concerned mostly with making a profit and get-

The governing committee of a Soviet collective farm meets to discuss production and management. During the 1920s, with his First Five-Year Plan, Stalin instituted a policy of farm collectivization in the Soviet Union in an attempt to move rural labor into the cities and to concentrate the country's resources in heavy industry.

Russian farmers break for lunch on a collective farm. The basic principle of communism is common ownership, and Stalin's farm collectivization was consistent with that principle in that one of its goals was to abolish private property.

ting rich. The proletariat, Marx believed, would eventually overthrow the capitalists through revolution, and thereafter private property would be abolished, thus ending the oppression of one class by another. A society without social classes, as the theory goes, would then use all production for satisfying human needs and not merely for capitalist profits.

Being a strict Marxist means being an atheist. Karl Marx called religion the opiate of the masses. Although Jaruzelski grew up in a deeply religious family and was educated by priests, he said his decision to reject Catholicism and declare himself an atheist is not that surprising. He explained his conversion in his 1987 interview with Zrnka Novak, which was published as a book in Poland. Jaruzelski said the daily religious services in the boarding school bored him, as they would many young teenagers, while the shock of the German invasion of Poland led him to question the existence of a righteous God.

"In my youngest years I was a firm believer. First communion, the first years of school. . . . My faith was very authentic. In the next stage, let's call it boyhood, I went to a school taught by Marianist priests. I was still a believer but an element of monotony was creeping in. Prayers in the morning, prayers in the evening, prayers before and after every meal, frequent Masses, confession, communion, retreats . . . It was at odds with my nature at that age. The daily demands overcame the authentic religious experience. . . .

"Then came the war years. The great shock that we all experienced and the conditions at that time led to a 'religious crack,' a passivity and indifference. After that various doubts began to grow. Before the war we were instilled with the belief that the Polish nation is cherished by God, that it is under his special care, and also that God is infinitely good, just, and . . . all powerful. In light of the military adversities and immense suffering of our nation, this did not hold water. And in general the idea that people, even innocent children, should have to suffer eternally for the original sin of our biblical forefathers, seemed to me at the time to be quite excessive and contrary to a morality of goodness, love and goodheartedness."

Jaruzelski's disillusionment with Catholicism during the war may be understandable, but it was not typical. If anything, Poles looked even more to the church as a source of hope and salvation in difficult times. Most Poles of his generation maintained a deep faith in God, and today more than 90 percent of Poles consider themselves Catholic. Most Poles also do not share the affinity for the Russians that Jaruzelski developed during the war. From the Nazi-Soviet Non-Aggression Pact in 1939 to the "liberation" of Poland in 1944–45, the Soviets did little

> *We have become a people who can live only in the imagination of what we believe to be the glorious past. When the present is too painful to contemplate, then we seek solace in our national folklore.*
> —anonymous Polish historian

> *Only one subject cannot be touched or shaken, and that is the principle of Poland's raison d'etre.*
> —WOJCIECH JARUZELSKI
> December 1986

to win themselves any friends in Poland. Jaruzelski may have been able to put aside old animosities and accept the Soviet Union as Poland's legitimate ally, but most Poles were not. Imposing the Soviet system on a fiercely Roman Catholic, anti-Communist, and anti-Russian population would be, as Stalin himself said, like "putting a saddle on a cow." The saddle just would not fit.

Stalin made his move in Poland and the other Eastern European countries in 1948. The heightened tensions between the Soviet Union and the United States, commonly referred to as the cold war, had increased so that Stalin, for national security reasons, wanted control over the countries that separated him from the West. In Poland, he demanded that the top leadership positions be filled either by Soviet advisers or Polish Communists who would obey his orders. Władysław Gomułka, the leader of the Polish Communist party, was not such a man. He was a dedicated Communist, but he had his own ideas about how communism should be introduced in Poland, and in Stalin's eyes that meant he had to go. Gomułka was forced to admit publicly that he had made serious mistakes as party leader. But Gomułka was lucky. Although he was arrested, he did not share the fate of discredited Communist leaders in the Soviet Union, who were often executed, and he would be released after Stalin's death and return to rule Poland for 14 years. Gomułka was replaced in 1948 as first secretary of the Communist party by Bolesław Bierut, a loyal follower of Stalin. During the eight years of Bierut's administration, the party would be subject to direct Soviet control.

Stalin wanted Poland and the other Soviet bloc countries to be Soviet satellites, with political, economic, and social systems based on the Soviet model. The Soviet-style communism that was imposed on Poland became known as Stalinism, modeled as it was on the totalitarian system that Stalin had created in his own country. The system was predicated on the Communist party having total control over the government, economy, and all aspects of social life. Communist rule was enforced by secret police, who infused an element of fear.

Poland's leaders controlled the economy through an enormous bureaucracy; decisions made at the top were passed down through the hierarchy to the factory managers. The state controlled what factories were built, what each factory would produce, and even to whom manufacturers would sell their products. Prices were also set by the government.

In 1948, Poland's economy was restructured to give priority to heavy industry. The state built giant factories and steel mills, hoping to increase the production of coal, iron, and steel as rapidly as possible. Consumer goods, such as clothes, appliances, and everyday household items, were neglected. One goal of the industrial development was to create a strong working class, the supposed backbone of the Communist workers' state.

Another motive of the rapid industrialization was to give the Soviet bloc the means to arm itself without having to rely on Western matériel. Stalin wanted a strong military in order to defend Communist rule in Eastern Europe, and top priority in Poland's restructured economy was given to the production of armaments. Conscription was introduced, and Poland's standing army grew to become the largest in Europe. Even today, with few exceptions, all Polish men are required to serve in the army.

Stalinism also meant changes in the countryside, where the majority of the population still lived on small family farms. Stalin thought the peasant

Stalin's collectivization policy was aimed at the annihilation of the *kulaks*, or private farmers. When the kulaks resisted his policy, Stalin declared an economic war on the Russian peasantry, ultimately causing the starvation of more than 5 million people during the 1930s.

A Polish electric plant. In the 1930s and 1940s, the Communist party gave top priority to the development of heavy industry throughout the Eastern bloc in an effort to intensify the production of coal, iron, steel, and, of course, armaments.

farmers, with their capitalist instincts and old-fashioned farming techniques, would block the development of a modern Communist state. Peasants were told to pool their land and form collective farms. Their pigs, cows, and chickens were also to be turned over to the collective farm.

The new Communist state, aiming for total control over society, tried to control education, culture, and the general flow of information. Books, movies, and newspapers were tightly censored to prohibit free expression of thought, and no criticism of the party or its policies was permitted. The state also tried to discredit the Catholic church and turn Poles away from religion. Writers, film directors, playwrights, poets, and artists were expected to use their creative talents to glorify Stalin, the socialist state, and the socialist working class.

Although Stalinism brought profound changes to Poland, it did not work the way it was supposed to in this historically anti-Communist and rebellious country. Efforts to collectivize the peasant farmers failed and ultimately antagonized the very people who would be needed to feed the growing urban working class. Resulting food shortages in the cities led to workers' riots and general social unrest. Stalin's efforts to discredit the church also backfired: The Catholic church, which for centuries had been closely tied to Poland's struggle for national independence, grew stronger as Poles rallied to defend it against the onslaught of the atheist government.

Then, on March 6, 1953, an official Soviet news release announced, "The heart of Joseph Stalin, Lenin's comrade-in-arms and inspired continuator of his work, wise leader and educator of the Communist party and the Soviet people, has stopped beating." When the news reached the work camps, which Stalin had filled with his detractors, prisoners wept with joy. A long, difficult period in history had come to an end, and a new era in the Soviet Union, and thus in Poland, was about to begin.

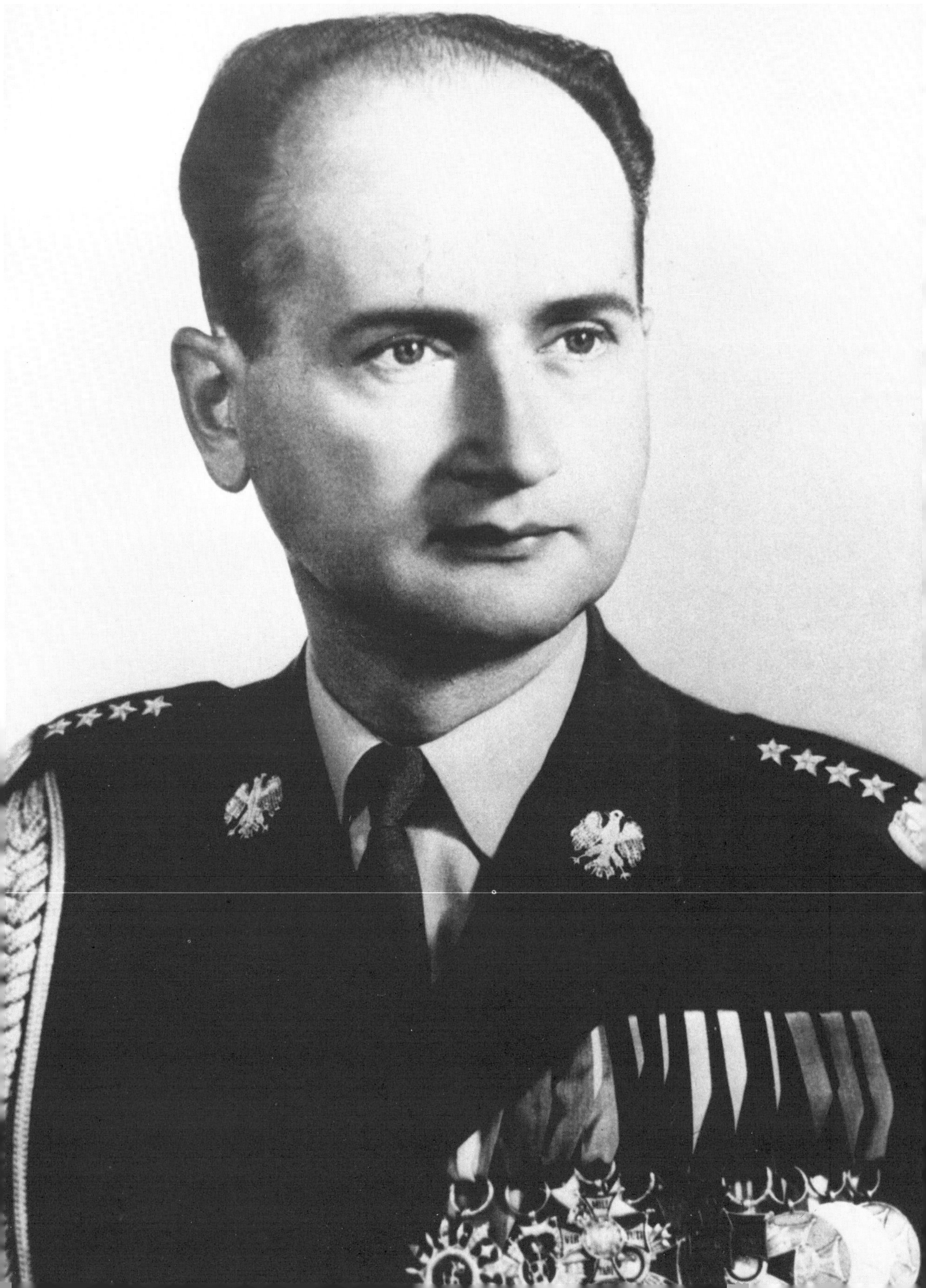

6
The Thaw

After Stalin's death, Poles began to claim the right to a more independent government. As the secret police were reined in and censorship was relaxed, people became less afraid to speak out for greater individual freedoms.

Stalinism had devastated Poland politically and economically. The men and women who filled the thousands of bureaucratic posts in government ministries had been appointed and promoted more for their party loyalty than for their ability to administer. Poor economic planning during the Stalin era had left Poland with coal mines, steel mills, and other heavy industries that were no longer profitable on the world market. The failures and atrocities of the Stalinist era quickly became apparent following the Soviet leader's death as people began to talk more freely, and this led to widespread social discontent.

The thaw that followed Stalin's death turned into a flood in 1956, when the new Soviet leader, Nikita Khrushchev, attacked Stalin and revealed his crimes for the first time in a "secret speech" at the 20th Congress of the Soviet Communist party.

What Poland needs above all is peace. The most vital interests of the Polish nation and State are vested in peace and détente, both in Europe and worldwide.
—WOJCIECH JARUZELSKI

Jaruzelski continued to climb steadily up through the Polish military ranks during the 1950s and 1960s. In July 1956, at the age of 33, he achieved the rank of general, and in 1960 he became Poland's chief political commissar.

Bolesław Bierut, the Stalinist Polish leader who was in Moscow for the congress, died there shortly after it ended. Although the cause of Bierut's death was given as heart failure, many suspected it was suicide. Bierut knew that the current denunciation of Stalin in the Soviet Union and that country's movement toward a more liberal political and social course would also occur in the satellite countries. The Stalinist leaders in Poland would be discredited, driven out of office, and possibly prosecuted for conspiring with Stalin. Some speculated that rather than face this likelihood, Bierut took his own life.

The disclosure of Stalinist crimes in Poland came as a shock to Poland's workers, who for 10 years had been told that they were building a new and better country, that their labors would be rewarded with better living conditions. Many had believed that through hard work and sacrifice they were creating a just and prosperous society. Then, in 1956, they were told not that prosperity was just around the corner, but that they were on the wrong road after all. The revelation that Stalin and his Polish followers had committed crimes against the people and led the country astray disillusioned and angered the Polish workers.

Discontent erupted in June, when workers in Poznan rioted in the streets. They carried banners saying Russians Go Home. Fighting broke out with the security police and the army. Even according to official figures, which tend to underestimate the magnitude of such incidents, 74 people were killed and 575 were injured in the course of 2 days. In need of a leader who had the support of the populace, the Poles turned to Gomułka. Although still a Communist, Gomułka was seen as a Polish nationalist, not a Soviet puppet. He promised the people a "Polish road to socialism."

The news that Poland's Communist leaders, without conferring with their Moscow overlords, were about to make Gomułka the new first secretary produced a panic in the Kremlin. Khrushchev and other top Soviet leaders flew to Warsaw, Soviet troops moved toward the Polish border, those Soviet

> *Gomulka became convinced that . . . Russia was prepared to settle the continuing problems of European security and Germany at the expense of Poland. His constant nightmare was that Poland's western territories . . . would be returned to Germany under an overall peace treaty.*
>
> —anonymous Polish politician

troops already stationed in Poland converged on the capital, and Soviet warships moved within sight of Gdansk. Still, the Poles did not back down. Polish troops were positioned along the roads into Warsaw. Workers also came to Gomułka's support. There were reports that blockades of overturned buses and tramcars were set up along roads, while trains were welded to tracks to block the railways.

The confrontation, dangerous while it lasted, was quickly resolved. Gomułka succeeded in convincing the Soviet leader that he was a loyal Communist and, like Khrushchev himself, was right in trying to overthrow the yoke of Stalinism and build a better, more just socialist system. The two leaders reached an understanding that fundamentally changed the relationship between their countries. Convinced that the unity of the bloc was not threatened, Khrushchev accepted Gomułka and his Polish road to socialism. Soviet advisers and military officers were sent home. The Central Committee elected Gomułka first secretary on October 21, 1956, and the Polish Communist party took control of Poland without direct supervision from Moscow.

In neighboring Hungary, the struggle for autonomy took a more violent turn. A full-scale revolution broke out in late October, when Imre Nagy formed

Polish tanks put down labor unrest in 1956. Workers took to the streets that June in Poznan, Poland, to protest the government's harsh, totalitarian treatment of the country's laborers. Nearly 600 people were killed or injured in the failed uprising.

The Polish Communist party leader Wladyslaw Gomulka (left) meets with Yugoslav president Tito in Slovenia, Yugoslavia, in the 1950s, a decade of political and social unrest throughout the Eastern bloc. Their meeting resulted in a declaration that drew sharp distinctions between their more open brand of communism and that of the Soviets.

a new coalition government and withdrew Hungary from the Warsaw Pact, thereby taking a first step toward establishing Hungarian independence. A few days later, Soviet troops stormed the capital city of Budapest, and the revolution was crushed. Thousands of people died during the invasion, and thousands more, including Nagy, were executed as the Soviets reasserted their control.

Meanwhile, Wojciech Jaruzelski was climbing steadily up through the ranks of the Polish army. Not long after completing his military schooling in Poland and the Soviet Union, he was appointed head of the army's Department of Military Academies, Schools, and Officers' Courses, a post that enabled him to lay the foundation of Poland's military education system. He was later chosen to head the Central Department of Battle Training.

Jaruzelski was promoted during the turmoil of 1956. In July, a month after the Poznan riots, Jaruzelski, at the age of 33, became one of Poland's youngest generals. In 1957 he moved to Szczecin, a port city on the Baltic Sea in the far northwest corner of Poland, where for the next three years he commanded the army's 12th Mechanized Division. It was during this time that he met Barbara Jaskólska, a ballet dancer. The two were married in Szczecin in 1960, and their daughter, Monika, was born in 1963.

In 1960, General Jaruzelski became Poland's chief political commissar when he was made head of the main political board of the Polish armed forces, an important post in the socialist defense system, which gave Jaruzelski considerable influence in Poland's military affairs. The assignment was a clear sign that he had earned the party's trust. He was promoted again in 1962 to the post of deputy minister of national defense, and in 1965, he was appointed chief of the general staff. In April 1968, now a two-star general, Jaruzelski was named minister of national defense and soon thereafter was made a three-star general. He would serve as minister of national defense for the next 15 years. As such, he was commander in chief of all the regular armed forces, a primarily administrative post.

Jaruzelski's promotion to defense minister in 1968 directly followed an anti-Semitic campaign in Poland, set off by student riots. The campaign, which reflected a complicated power struggle in the upper echelons of the party, proved to be one of the most shameful episodes in the country's postwar history.

The campaign was some party leaders' way of dealing with growing opposition to the party, which had come mainly from Polish intellectuals, including many who had supported Gomułka in the beginning, and younger Poles, who were frustrated by increasing economic difficulties and disturbed by the party's treatment of respected writers and scholars. Now they were disillusioned with Gomułka, who

Soviet tanks patrol the streets of Budapest, Hungary, in 1956. In October of that year, Hungarians made a bid for their independence from the Soviet Union by staging an uprising, but after only a few days the Soviets brutally crushed the revolt.

no longer seemed to champion the promise of a more democratic political system, rational economic reform, or greater cultural freedom.

Intellectuals, many of them party members, began calling for greater tolerance of artistic creativity and freedom of expression, but the party refused to relax censorship and expelled members who challenged the orthodox line. The crisis came when the government closed down a production at the National Theater in Warsaw of *Forefathers' Eve*, a play by the 19th-century poet and dramatist Adam Mickiewicz about Poland's struggle for independence from the Russian czar. The audiences loudly cheered the lines deriding the Russian despots. After the final performance on January 30, students from the University of Warsaw marched from the theater to a monument to Mickiewicz in the center of the city. The police were waiting for them, and the students were beaten and arrested. Tensions continued to rise throughout the next month, and a mass rally at the university on March 8 was broken up violently by police. Hundreds of students were arrested and later expelled from the university. Professors who supported them lost their jobs.

The crisis was blamed on a group of intellectuals, many of whom were Jewish. The Jews who survived the Holocaust and remained in Poland after the war were a small but influential community. Many intellectuals and senior party officials, including a number close to Gomułka, were Jewish. A vicious

As commander of the Polish army's Twelfth Mechanized Division, in 1957 Jaruzelski (center) was stationed in Szczecin, a port city on the Baltic coast. In 1962, he became deputy minister of national defense, and in 1965 he was named chief of the general staff.

campaign of harassment and humiliation was launched against them. Hundreds of Jewish leaders were expelled from the party and fired from their jobs, while others — Jewish and non-Jewish — left voluntarily in disgust. Edward Ochab, a distinguished Communist who had served as first secretary of the party in the interim between Bierut's death and Gomułka's appointment, protested the anti-Semitic campaign by leaving his seat in the Politburo and resigning as chairman of the Council of State. He was not Jewish, but he was appalled by the campaign. The Sejm accepted Ochab's resignation as head of state and appointed Defense Minister Marian Spychalski to take his place. This opened the door for Jaruzelski to become the next defense minister.

Meanwhile, attempts to liberalize Czechoslovakia had ended in catastrophe. There, the challenge to Soviet orthodoxy was led by the Communist party, which under the new leadership of Alexander Dubček was championing extremely liberal policies, including the abolition of censorship. When Soviet troops invaded Czechoslovakia in August 1968, they were backed up by soldiers from Poland and other Warsaw Pact countries. As the new defense minister, Jaruzelski must have helped plan the invasion of Poland's southern neighbor.

The 1960s were a turning point for some of contemporary Poland's most prominent opposition intellectuals. Jacek Kuron, once a fervent young Marxist, was kicked out of the party in 1964 and sentenced to prison for three years after criticizing the state in "An Open Letter to the Party." Adam Michnik, one of the leaders of the student protests, was expelled from the university in 1968. The following year he was charged with belonging to an underground organization and sentenced to three years in prison. These were the first of many prison terms these dissidents and others like them would receive for their opposition to Communist rule.

At this time, intellectuals who fought for change in Poland received no active support from the working class. Workers resented intellectuals for their earlier support of the Communist state, and many

> *After the Russian invasion of 1968, every Czech was confronted with the thought that his nation could be quietly erased from Europe.*
> —MILAN KUNDERA
> Czech writer

Defiant Czech patriots cruise the streets of Prague, Czechoslovakia, waving Czech flags at Soviet tanks in the aftermath of Prague Spring, the uprising that set off a brief period of political ferment in Czechoslovakia in 1968. The Soviets, who have controlled Czechoslovakia since 1948, quashed the uprising.

believed at least partially the government's anti-Semitic slander. Moreover, the intellectuals were fighting for freedom of speech, a guarantee of basic civil rights, and other lofty principles. They were less concerned with workers' wages and food shortages, the basic demands that had sent workers into the streets in 1956.

In 1970, Gomułka decided to raise food prices about 20 percent only 2 weeks before Christmas, a time when Polish families usually stock their shelves for the traditional Christmas Eve feast. Workers, already frustrated by their low living standards, were furious. The rebellion was strongest in Gdansk, where thousands of shipyard workers went on strike and rioted in the streets. They set fire to the local party headquarters and the central train station.

The government reacted with force, authorizing the police and army to open fire on workers. According to official figures, and unofficial counts run much higher, 45 workers were killed and almost 1,000 were injured in a week of fighting that spread from Gdansk to other cities on the Baltic coast. Policemen and soldiers also suffered casualties; official figures list 3 dead and 600 injured. It was clearly Gomułka's decision to use force rather than negotiate with the workers. What is not clear is whether by doing so he disregarded the advice of his defense minister. Many Poles believe the orders to fire on Polish workers were given against Jaruzelski's will and without his direct authority.

The riots stopped after a week, but strikes broke out throughout Poland. In the beginning, workers had demanded wage increases and price freezes, but after the government sent Poles to shoot Poles and the conflict turned bloody, workers' demands became more political. In 1970, the call for independent trade unions was first heard among shipyard workers on the Baltic coast. It would take 10 years for their call to be answered.

The riots drove Władysław Gomułka out of office and brought to power a new group of men led by Edward Gierek, the local party leader in the coal-mining region of Silesia. On December 20, Gierek was elected first secretary of the party. One beneficiary of the shift in power was Wojciech Jaruzelski, who had been a member of the Central Committee since 1964. He became a candidate, or nonvoting, member of the Politburo soon after Gierek took power and a full member a year later. The move into

A Polish tank imposes its powerful presence in the streets of Gdansk. In 1970, when the Polish government raised food prices, workers went on strike in several major Polish cities. Rioting ensued, and the government responded with force, killing more than 40 workers and injuring as many as 1,000 others.

> *Gierek was always very much Moscow's man.*
> —STEWART STEVEN
> English writer

the top ranks of the party leadership put him in a position to play a stronger political as well as military role in Poland.

Gierek and other top officials went to the Baltic coast to meet with striking workers. Jaruzelski was among those who supported the decision to initiate direct negotiations with the workers. It was the first time the party had ever done that, and it worked. Gierek stood before the workers and pleaded with them for their support. A coal miner by trade, he told them he was a worker, too, and that he needed their help to save Poland. "I say to you, help us, help me," Gierek said at the shipyard. "I am only a worker like you . . . but now, and I tell you this in all solemnity as a Pole and as a communist, the fate of our nation and the cause of socialism are in the balance." The workers were impressed that Gierek had come to them and were willing to give the new party leader a chance. They responded to his appeal by shouting *Pomozemy*, which means "We will help," and they agreed to go back to work.

At that point, Gierek refused to rescind the food price rises, but a couple of months later, when strikes again started breaking out, he backed down and restored the old prices. Although the decision to increase prices right before Christmas showed political ineptitude, Polish leaders had had sound economic reasons for wanting to raise food prices. Grocery stores, like most businesses, were run by the state, and for years food had been heavily subsidized to keep prices low. This was done so that no one in the socialist state should go hungry, but it meant that the state sold food for less than it cost to produce. The subsidies created ridiculous situations. For example, it became cheaper for farmers to sell their grain to the state and then buy bread, sold at low subsidized prices, to feed their pigs. This may have been cheaper for farmers, but it was an expensive and wasteful situation for Poland. Even so, the state was not able or willing to pay farmers enough for their products to cover the steadily rising costs of production, which meant that farmers had little incentive to grow more crops or raise more livestock. Compounding the problem was that at the

Jaruzelski is presented with a commemorative photo album tracing the history of the Polish armed forces by First Secretary Gomułka in February 1970. The rioting and widespread discontent of that year forced Gomułka to resign his post as head of the Polish Communist party.

subsidized prices people wanted to buy more food than was available. Shortages of meat and dairy products were getting worse. The price rises were designed to bring supply and demand more into balance.

The events of 1970 and 1971 gave the workers a hint of their potential power. They had overthrown a government, brought new leaders to their door for direct negotiations, and in the end succeeded in preventing a price increase. The events also confirmed a split in Polish opposition to the Communist government that had been manifest in 1968, when students and intellectuals had received no support from workers in their protests against censorship and other restrictions of civil rights. In 1970, when workers called on students to join their demonstrations against price rises, the students stayed inside. This split between workers and intellectuals would have to be bridged if Poles were to stand a chance of successfully challenging Communist rule. The 1970s and beyond promised to be a struggle but offered a chance for all Poles to come together and fight for a freer, more democratic society.

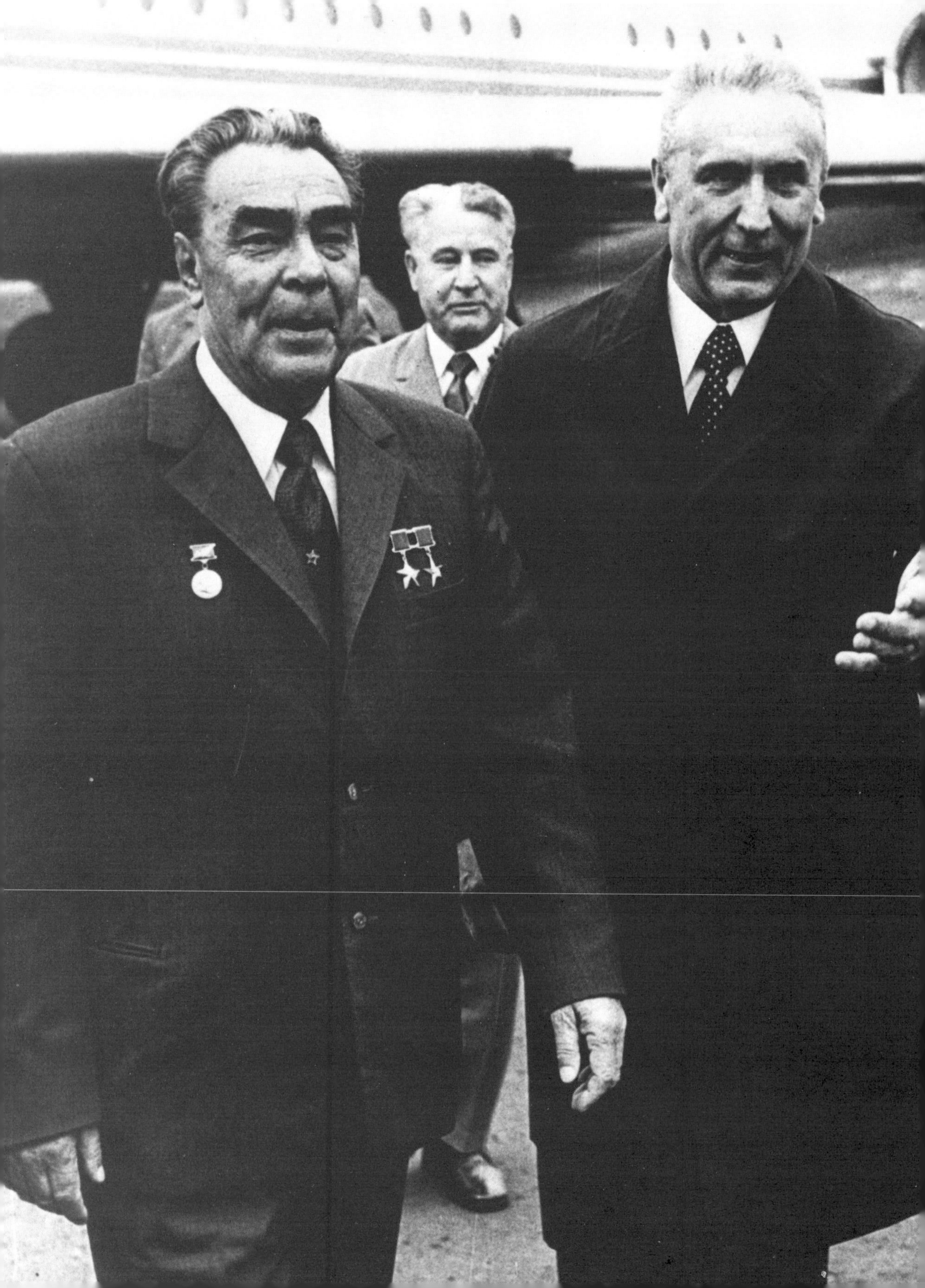

7
The Cycle of Unrest

Edward Gierek set out on a bold path to modernize Poland's economy and win workers' support for his Communist government. Labor unrest in 1970 had toppled the regime of his predecessor, Władysław Gomułka, and he wanted to prevent the same thing from happening to him.

Gierek's strategy was to modernize Polish industry as rapidly as possible by using technology and equipment imported from the United States and Western Europe. The imports, which also included food and consumer goods, were paid for with credits from Western banks and governments, while exports from the new and improved Polish industries were expected to earn enough hard currency to pay back the loans. (Poland's currency — the *zloty* — is soft, or not convertible, having no value outside of Poland.) However, Gierek's strategy was poorly implemented: Money borrowed from the West was pumped into outdated heavy industries, most notably steel and shipbuilding. While steel plants in the United States were shutting down, mills in Poland were being expanded. As a result, wages and the demand for consumer goods grew much faster than planned. So did workers' expectations for a better future.

> *Solidarity was born at the precise moment when the shipyard strike [at Gdansk] evolved from a local success in the shipyard to a strike in support of other factories . . . large and small, in need of our protection.*
> —LECH WALESA
> on the advent of Solidarity

Soviet leader Leonid Brezhnev meets with Edward Gierek, Gomulka's successor as first secretary of the Polish Communist party. The Gierek regime tried to lay a new emphasis on housing and consumer goods and instituted a program for industrial expansion financed by Western governments.

Poles clamor for vodka, a rare and relatively expensive commodity in Poland. During the early 1970s, the reforms of the Gierek regime created an illusion of prosperity with an infusion of Western money. When the loans came due, however, the Polish economy sputtered, and the Polish people realized the emptiness of the government's promises.

The illusion of prosperity was short lived. Though the standard of living rose rapidly during the early 1970s, the Polish economy began a downward spiral midway through that decade. As the Western loans came due, it was clear that Poland was not going to be able to repay the money. Poland's problems were compounded by an oil crisis that depressed the world market and drove interest rates sky high. Poland had to borrow more money just to pay interest on its debts. Food, medicine, shoes, and other household items began disappearing from store shelves. Housing construction slowed. The government's failures and false promises became increasingly clear to the population. Moreover, corruption among the party elite became more visible as top officials appropriated state funds to enrich their own lives.

Then, in June 1976, without warning or consulting the workers, the government announced that prices would go up about 70 percent for meat and 35 percent for cheese and butter, while the price of sugar would double. Workers, predictably, were not pleased with the news.

Unlike in capitalist countries, where the prices of goods and services are determined by somewhat intangible market forces, in a centrally planned economy such as Poland's, the state has the power to set prices. Consequently, when prices increase abrubtly, the government is blamed.

The day after the price increases were announced, workers throughout Poland went on strike. As in 1970, the outbreak was not just about prices, but about poor working conditions and the continued lack of unions or councils to represent the workers on policy matters. Workers saw their standard of living deteriorate while corrupt communist officials bought food in special stores and built villas in the country. Baltic shipyard workers again began organizing committees and drawing up lists of demands. Several thousand workers at the Ursus tractor factory near Warsaw protested by marching to the main east-west railway line and blocking the tracks. Workers demonstrated their potential for disrupting communication between the Soviet Union and its military forces in East Germany. Workers in Radom, southwest of Warsaw, set fire to party headquarters there.

As in 1971, the government backed down and rescinded the price increases. The workers had won again, much more quickly this time, but they would be punished for their victory. Police and security forces were ordered to take reprisal. They made workers run what they so spitefully called the "path of health," a gauntlet through two lines of police who hit them with batons as they passed by. Thousands of workers were fired from their jobs for their roles in the strikes, and many were arrested.

It was during the trials of the Ursus and Radom workers that the bond between workers and intellectuals was forged. The workers, who were facing stiff jail sentences, had no means of defending themselves in court, and a group of intellectuals came to their assistance by establishing the Workers Defense Committee, now known by its Polish initials KOR. Some of KOR's members, such as Jacek Kuron and Adam Michnik, were veterans of the student protests in 1968. KOR's first aim was to raise money to provide legal defense for the workers and to support the families of workers while they

Under the direction of Cardinal Stefan Wyszynski during the 1970s, the Polish Catholic church played a more active role in Polish political affairs than it had in the recent past, taking a stand on important issues and opening a dialogue with Jews, Marxists, and other non-Catholics.

were in jail. But KOR also succeeded in stirring up artists and writers who had retreated after the 1968 debacle and encouraged them to become involved in opposition activity. After KOR was formed, more and more intellectuals dared to speak out against the communist government. Uncensored, or underground, publications began to flourish. Journals, newsletters, and translations of prohibited Polish and Western books, including George Orwell's *Animal Farm*, were secretly printed and sold. Copies were eagerly read and then passed on.

Next the Catholic church got into the action. In the second half of the 1970s the church began to play a more active political role in Poland; under Stefan Cardinal Wyszynski the church started to take a stand on important social issues, expanding its concern beyond strictly religious matters. Doors began to open up between the church and opposition intellectuals, many of whom were Marxists, Jews, and other non-Catholics who had traditionally viewed the church as a conservative, intolerant institution. Both groups were coming to realize that they shared common goals and that each would be stronger if they worked together.

In October 1978, Karol Cardinal Wojtyla, archbishop of Kraków, was elected pope. He was the first Pole and the first non-Italian in 500 years to be chosen for the highest post in the Roman Catholic church, and his election filled Poles with joy and a

Cardinal Karol Wojtyla became Pope John Paul II in October 1978. His papacy has been a controversial one: He has denounced capitalist and communist governments alike for exploiting people and violating their rights while harshly criticizing progressive elements within the church.

Solidarity leader Lech Walesa is hoisted above the Lenin Shipyard fence at a rally of the labor union coalition in Gdansk in 1980, the year it was founded.

sense of national pride. When Pope John Paul II returned to Poland in June 1979, Poles thronged the streets. Between one-fourth and one-fifth of the population turned out to meet the pope on his pilgrimage through Poland. As many as 2 million gathered for his farewell ceremony in an open meadow outside Kraków.

In 1980, workers, intellectuals, and the Catholic church joined forces and united the Polish people under one banner. Standing together, tens of thousands strong, Poles understood that they formed a society with shared values and that those values were not necessarily those that had been expounded from the pulpit of the Politburo for the past 30 years. Poles experienced a renewed hope and self-confidence. When in the summer of 1980 the government once again tried to raise food prices, it was met not

Lech Walesa (with mustache) and Polish vice prime minister Mieczyslaw Jagielski sign the Gdansk Agreement in August 1980. The most significant step for Polish labor in 35 years, the agreement provided for the legal establishment of independent trade unions.

by violent outbursts and uncontrolled street riots but by the determined opposition of a united people. They called their movement Solidarność, or Solidarity.

On August 14, 1980, workers in the Lenin Shipyard in Gdansk demanded a cost-of-living pay raise, and by that evening thousands of workers had gathered inside the shipyard gates. In an effort to avoid a strike, the manager of the yard told the workers that if they went back to their jobs he would consider their demand. The manager's offer was preempted, however, when Lech Walesa, an electrician who would become the leader of Solidarity, was lifted over the fence that encircled the shipyard. Walesa called for an occupation strike, and the workers cheered him on.

The workers established a strike committee and drew up a list of demands. Influenced by KOR and the lessons of 1970, workers were no longer limiting themselves to economic concerns, and their list of demands, which eventually grew to 21, included the abolition of censorship, release of political prisoners, access to mass media, the right to strike, and above all the right to establish free trade unions. Hundreds of other factories joined the strike, and the Inter-Factory Strike Committee (MKS) was formed to negotiate for all of them.

Top-level party officials came from Warsaw to negotiate with the workers, who called in a group of intellectuals — economists, sociologists, historians, some members of Catholic intellectual groups, and others associated with KOR — to serve as their advisers. The negotiations were broadcast over loudspeakers to the 6,000 workers who remained inside the shipyard during the occupation strike. Crowds waiting anxiously for news of the negotiations gathered outside the gate, which Solidarity supporters had decorated with flowers, religious icons, and portraits of the pope.

The talks continued for two weeks. The government negotiators were gradually acquiescing to workers' demands, but then on August 29 they announced that they were not coming to the shipyard that day. The talks had been stalled by a political crisis in Warsaw. Hard-line members of the Polish Politburo were demanding that the workers' revolt be stopped before it was out of control; they wanted to declare a state of emergency and call in the army to bust the strikes. Still, Gierek stood firm on his decision to solve the crisis through negotiation, and he was backed by Jaruzelski and Stanislaw Kania, who was in charge of security forces. The negotiators returned to the table the next day and on Sunday, August 31, the Gdansk Agreement was signed.

Solidarity was born in the Lenin Shipyard, and grew into a nationwide movement as delegates of strike committees from every province joined together to form the National Coordinating Committee of the New Independent Self-governing Trades Union (NSZZ). Though Solidarity started as an organization to represent workers and defend their rights, it soon became a powerful movement for freedom and independence that reached all sectors of society.

Gierek did not last long after Solidarity was formed. On the morning of September 5, the Sejm met to confirm the appointment of Józef Pinkowski

> *The extremist forces in Solidarity are forming a counter-government, motivated by dictatorial aspirations. The mass of its members are forced to submit to the will of its leaders in order to further their ambitions and plans. They remain unaware of the gruesome game into which they are being drawn.*
> —WOJCIECH JARUZELSKI
> in a speech before the Sejm, October 30, 1981

as prime minister. Gierek was not present, which was odd because the first secretary customarily introduced the party's choice for prime minister. During Pinkowski's speech, a message was delivered to Defense Minister Jaruzelski and Interior Minister Stanislaw Kowalczyk. They immediately left the parliament chamber. By afternoon the news was out that Gierek had had a heart attack while on his way to the Sejm that morning. Party leaders did not wait to see whether Gierek would recover: In a meeting late that night they picked Stanislaw Kania to become the new first secretary.

A historical agreement had been signed between the government and Solidarity in Gdansk, but the signature of the government negotiator did not guarantee that the provisions of the agreement would be honored throughout Poland. In the months that followed, Solidarity, under the leadership of Lech Walesa, who was elected chairman of the labor union, tried to have those provisions made into law, but the government obstructed its efforts, afraid for either economic or political reasons to honor the agreement. Tensions began to build and strikes again broke out. The party, in desperate need of inspired leadership, looked to Jaruzelski: He was made Poland's prime minister February 9, 1981. He also retained his post as defense minister.

A four-star general since 1973, Jaruzelski was the first military commander to become the head of a Soviet bloc country. Poles were startled but impressed. The army in Poland was well respected. Unlike the security forces and riot police, recruited to do the dirty work of the Communist state, the conscript army was made up of everyone's sons and brothers. Jaruzelski benefited from the patriotic feelings Poles still had for the military, which traditionally had fought to protect Poland's independence. In addition, the general was liked because he was believed to have opposed the use of force against striking workers in the past, and he was said to favor a political solution to the crisis in 1981. Jaruzelski brought in Mieczyslaw Rakowski to be his deputy prime minister and gave him the job of negotiating with Solidarity. The most volatile

---

Workers were to be silent, or if from time to time they were allowed to speak, it had to be according to a scenario imposed from above.
—Polish worker at the Lenin Shipyard in Gdansk

strikes were settled and tensions were eased, but only temporarily.

The most serious crisis since August 1980 began in Bydgoszcz on March 19, 1981, when police brutally beat protesters who were calling for the legalization of Rural Solidarity, a union that had been formed to protect the interests of private farmers. Solidarity demanded not only that Rural Solidarity be legalized but that those responsible for the beatings be prosecuted. The union threatened a general strike if its demands were not met by March 31. On March 27, Solidarity showed its strength by calling a four-hour warning strike. The situation was tense. Workers throughout Poland began to prepare for the work stoppage by stockpiling food and supplies in factories. Party hard-liners wanted to declare a state of emergency and call in the army to

Jaruzelski (far left) and other members of the Gierek government make a public appearance in 1979. Only days after the Gdansk Agreement was signed, Gierek was replaced by Stanislaw Kania as first secretary of the Polish Communist party.

put an end to Solidarity once and for all, but Jaruzelski and Kania managed to head them off. Meanwhile, Warsaw Pact troops were holding maneuvers on Polish soil, and Western governments were issuing warnings of a Soviet intervention. At the last minute, the crisis was averted when Walesa and Rakowski reached an agreement that suspended the strike.

The Bydgoszcz Crisis, as it was called, and the events of the following months increased the anxiety of Soviet leaders. In June they sent a threatening letter to Warsaw that pointed the finger at Kania and Jaruzelski, who they said were proving incapable of leading Poland out of the crisis. The Polish Communist party, however, rallied around its two

Jaruzelski, who was named Poland's prime minister in February 1981, meets with First Secretary Stanislaw Kania at the Monument of Heroes in Warsaw that year.

leaders and reelected them to their top posts at the Ninth Party Congress the next month. But the Soviet message had been clear, and Polish leaders knew they had to watch their step.

From the Soviets' point of view, the most dangerous aspect of the Polish crisis was the resultant weakening of the Polish Communist party. The enthusiasm generated by Solidarity clearly pointed up the failure of the party to govern Poland. Even party members had lost confidence in the party: As many as 1 million of its 3 million members joined Solidarity. Despite attempts to revitalize it during the summer of 1981, the party showed little new direction and made no progress either toward coming to

Jaruzelski (center) observes Warsaw Pact troop maneuvers with other Eastern bloc generals in Poland in March 1981. While the troops put on a show, a general workers' strike threatened to cripple the Polish economy, and the Polish hard-liners warned of a state of emergency.

Police patrol the streets of a small town in central Poland while women offer dry goods for sale to passersby. Jaruzelski claims that in addition to the serious economic decline in Poland during the 1980s, Solidarity's intransigence made the declaration of martial law necessary.

terms with Solidarity or devising an economic recovery program. The economy continued to decline. Rationing was introduced, but even so there were shortages, and people had to stand in line, often for hours, to buy basic goods such as sugar and soap. According to government figures, the national income declined 13 percent in 1981, while the foreign debt grew to $24.5 billion. It was the third consecutive year of negative growth.

In the beginning, Solidarity was unwilling to play a role in economic reform, insisting it was only a trade union, its job strictly to defend workers' interests. By the summer of 1981, however, workers saw that the party was doing nothing to stop the economy's downward spiral, and they looked to the

Solidarity leadership to take positive action. Solidarity changed its position and said it would be willing to work with the government to save the economy but only if the union was given some control over the design and implementation of economic reform programs.

Talks were held between representatives of Solidarity and the government, but the government, represented by Rakowski, was unwilling to share power with Solidarity. It wanted to incorporate Solidarity into the Communist state as a consultative body, which meant Solidarity was being asked to share responsibility for the country's economic and social problems without having the means to help correct them. All crucial decisions would still be made by the party. After breaking down in early August, the talks resumed in November, but the government's position had not substantially changed: Jaruzelski's administration was simply unwilling to collaborate with Solidarity on economic reform.

There was also discussion at this time among Solidarity members of creating a second chamber of the Sejm. This second parliamentary chamber, whose members would be freely elected as genuine representatives of Polish society, would function together with the existing chamber, which was controlled by the Communist party. The government rejected Solidarity's proposal.

General Jaruzelski replaced Kania as first secretary of the Communist party on October 18, and less than two months later he imposed martial law, thereby forcing Solidarity underground. It is not known when Jaruzelski made the decision to declare Poland in a "state of war," though the evidence suggests it was sometime in the fall of 1981. During the spring and summer, it appeared as if Jaruzelski still hoped to find a way of controlling Solidarity without calling in the army. What also is not known is whether Jaruzelski was ever forced to choose between an internal crackdown and Soviet intervention. Jaruzelski has insisted it was a purely Polish decision, but in any event he has been held responsible.

40 LAT PRL

8
Hard Work and Perseverance

When General Wojciech Jaruzelski crushed Solidarity, he crushed the hopes and dreams of many Poles. Despite the economic crisis, people had been optimistic and had believed they had a chance to build a more democratic society. But Jaruzelski left his countrymen facing only empty store shelves and the cold, gray winter that lay ahead. The soldiers on street corners were a grim reminder to Poles that they lived in a Soviet-dominated police state.

The mood in Poland after martial law was imposed was one of despair. Many Poles who were out of the country at the time chose not to return, and among those who sought political asylum were Poland's ambassadors to the United States and Japan. Later, when the borders were opened up, tourists left Poland but did not come back. Sailors jumped ship and swam for freer shores. The disillusioned included not only Solidarity supporters, but thousands of party members who turned in their membership cards, saying they had lost faith in socialism in Poland.

> *Wojciech Jaruzelski is . . . an idealist who looks for pragmatic as well as ideological solutions to problems. In himself he is austere and self-disciplined, but in his dealings with others he looks for conciliation rather than confrontation.*
> —ROBERT MAXWELL
> English publisher and writer

The festivities seem to have eluded this Warsaw souvenir vendor as she displays her wares in 1984 at the 40th anniversary celebration of Communist rule in Poland. Her expression reflects, among other things, the frustration and despair that characterized the mood in Poland after the imposition of martial law in 1981.

The West, especially the United States, condemned the Polish government for declaring martial law and putting many of its citizens in prison cells to await uncertain futures. The U.S. government imposed a number of stiff economic sanctions on Poland, including the withdrawal of most-favored-nation trade status and the denial of official credit to the country.

When a country loses its most-favored-nation trade status — in practice a status granted to most nations and rarely withdrawn — goods from that country are subject to much higher import tariffs on the American market. The sanction was effective: Polish exports to the United States dropped from about $450 million in 1980 to about $250 million a year later, as American consumers refused to pay higher prices for Polish exports. The denial of official credit meant that Polish trade representatives

In a pointed but fairly innocuous display of discontent, a Warsaw man leads his poodle through the city square behind the backs of unsuspecting police. To protest the imposition of martial law, many Poles walked their dogs each day during the television broadcast of the evening news.

could only buy American products with cash, an arrangement so impractical that trade with the United States was rendered extremely difficult. The United States also punished Poland by denying its fishing vessels the right to fish in American waters and forbidding its airline, LOT, to land planes at American airports.

In the battle for the minds of Poles, the party was losing. During martial law, many Poles took to walking their dogs during the evening news as a sign of protest. Many actors and entertainers boycotted the government-run television stations, sacrificing their incomes rather than condone the hated military regime. Meanwhile, a vast underground culture was thriving. Many newspapers, journals, and books were published clandestinely and widely distributed. As the police raided one underground printing shop, another would spring up across

Warsaw activists grasp at political pamphlets in 1981. During martial law, underground culture thrived: Political materials were published secretly and distributed in cities and towns throughout Poland, while plays, concerts, and lectures took place behind the closed doors of private residences.

town. Banned theater productions, concerts, and lectures were held in private apartments and in church basements.

In subsequent years, Jaruzelski was able to consolidate his own position in the Communist party, but winning society's confidence and solving the economic crisis remained beyond his grasp. Poland was caught in a desperate circle of poverty: Poles had lost confidence in the government because of its poor handling of the economy, the economic reforms necessary to bring about a recovery would require austerity measures, but the people would not go along with such measures because they had lost confidence in the government. In the past, government-instituted price rises had led to strikes, not economic renewal. Why should people trust a government that was leading the country further into poverty? Moreover, why should the Polish people support a government in which they had no voice?

Jaruzelski felt secure enough in October 1982 to ban Solidarity, which had technically only been "under suspension." Martial law was suspended in December 1982, a year after it was imposed, and finally lifted in July 1983, but Poles did not celebrate. Little had changed. Many of the tighter controls had simply been made into new laws, the economy was a disaster, and people were still in prison because of their political beliefs. A limited amnesty was granted that year, and more than 1,000 political prisoners were released, but the amnesty did not extend to the more well known Solidarity activists and many of those released were re-arrested within months.

After martial law was lifted, Jaruzelski relinquished his government positions. He gave up the position of defense minister in November 1983 and two years later resigned as prime minister to become chairman of the Council of State, a collective presidency. However, through special decrees by parliament and the Council of State, Jaruzelski maintained his role as supreme commander of the Polish armed forces. As Communist party leader and commander in chief, he still held the reins of power while turning the day-to-day administration over to others.

> *We shall conquer with unity.*
> —Polish shipyard workers

Jaruzelski addresses the Polish parliament in July 1982. In December of that year martial law was suspended, but it would not be lifted entirely until July 1983, after a visit to Poland by Pope John Paul II.

Jaruzelski faced some of his stiffest opposition from within the party, as illustrated by the murder of a pro-Solidarity priest in October 1984. The murder of Father Jerzy Popieluszko, who was abducted and beaten to death by secret police, was considered a provocation against Jaruzelski. Many believed that police had acted on the orders of hard-line members of the party who were frustrated by the tolerance shown to the outspoken priest and others like him by Jaruzelski and the more moderate party leaders. The murder was designed to discredit Jaruzelski at a time when he was taking steps toward some conciliation between the government and Solidarity, and between Poland and the West. Jaruzelski was able to turn Popieluszko's murder to his partial advantage when he allowed the public trial

Jerzy Popieluszko, a Polish clergyman and pro-Solidarity activist, was beaten to death by secret police in October 1984. His murder may have been ordered by party hard-liners in an attempt to discredit Jaruzelski, who had of late taken an increasingly moderate view of Solidarity demands.

of four secret policemen accused of killing the priest. It was the first time a Communist country had publicly prosecuted members of the security forces for killing a dissident.

As time went on, active mass support for Solidarity diminished. Calls for strikes and demonstrations were heeded by fewer and fewer. The public attitude toward Jaruzelski seemed to be changing, too. Poles still had little affection for him, but there was increasing respect for his intelligence and political savvy. His release of about 650 Solidarity detainees under a second amnesty, in July 1984, was well received in Poland and the West. The United States responded by lifting some of the economic restrictions it had placed on trade with Poland.

Jaruzelski's position within the party was strengthened at the 10th Party Congress in July 1986. He was reelected first secretary and also succeeded in eliminating his political rivals in the party leadership. Nine new members were named to the

15-member Politburo, which now included Jaruzelski, General Czeslaw Kiszczak, and two other army generals. Never had a Communist party had so many military people in positions of power. Jaruzelski appointed journalists as well: One of his top advisers, Wieslaw Gornicki, was once a foreign correspondent in the United States; one of the new members of the Politburo, Mieczyslaw Rakowski, who had negotiated with Solidarity in 1981, had been the editor of a political weekly.

Jaruzelski also received a strong endorsement from the new Soviet leader at the Party Congress. Mikhail Gorbachev had become first secretary in 1985, the third since Leonid Brezhnev died in November 1982. In his speech at the Polish congress, Gorbachev praised Jaruzelski for declaring martial law and thereby sparing the Soviet Union from the kind of decisions it had to make in Hungary in 1956 and Czechoslovakia in 1968.

With Solidarity suppressed and his own position secure, Jaruzelski turned his attention to the economy. An economic reform program begun in 1982 had failed miserably, and serious efforts to revive the economy were long overdue. His first move was to improve relations with Western governments.

Relations with Western nations, especially the United States, had not been good. The conditions the United States had given for lifting the sanctions — the freeing of political prisoners and an opening up of dialogue with Solidarity — were the same measures that would win Jaruzelski favor from Polish society. When the Polish leader came to New York to address the United Nations General Assembly in September 1985, U.S. government officials refused to meet with him because of the recent increase in the number of political arrests in Poland. Many of those who had been released under the amnesty were back in jail.

Jaruzelski took Poles by surprise when he announced a general amnesty in September 1986. All political prisoners were released from jail, and Jaruzelski said Poland would no longer imprison people for their political views. Jaruzelski also created the Consultative Council, an advisory board to

> *Jaruzelski wore a rather worried look. A confrontation with a real worker at the head of a big political movement was something unprecedented for him.*
> —LECH WALESA
> on his first meeting with Jaruzelski

Archbishop Józef Glemp (center), head of the Polish Roman Catholic church, played a major role in Poland's relations with the United States. In January 1987, he successfully appealed to a U.S. diplomat to relieve Poland from U.S. trade sanctions that had been in effect since the martial law period.

the government, but he was unable to persuade prominent Solidarity members or Catholic leaders to join. Solidarity, which considered the council a ploy designed only to give Western governments the impression that democratic reforms were taking place, dismissed it as a sham. Jaruzelski's next step toward at least the appearance of national reconciliation was to ease censorship. Criticism of government policies was not only permitted but encouraged, while films that had been shelved because of their political content were allowed to be released.

Jaruzelski's efforts got results. He was invited to Rome in January 1987 and welcomed for the first time on an official visit to the West. Later that month, U.S. deputy secretary of state John Whitehead arrived in Warsaw, the first senior U.S. official to visit Poland since martial law was declared. Whitehead liked what he saw, and while he was there, Archbishop Józef Glemp and Lech Walesa appealed to him to have the remaining economic sanctions on Poland lifted. They said the sanctions were hurting the Polish people and giving the government an excuse for its poor economic performance.

The sanctions were lifted in February, but Western governments and banks were still in no hurry to lend money to Poland. Without economic reforms, they had no guarantee that the money would not be wasted as it had been in the 1970s. Jaruzelski decided the time was right to move ahead with an economic reform program, and, in a national referendum held at the end of 1987, he asked the Polish people to approve the government plan even though it would mean they would have to tighten their belts and accept sharp price increases. Prices of basic foods would go up as much as 110 percent. The reasoning was that Poland could no longer afford the immense cost of subsidies, which the Communist government had used for decades to fulfill the promise of a just society in which basic goods and services, such as food, housing, education, and health care, were available to everyone.

It was the first real election held since the Communist government came to power, and Poles rejected the government plan by a narrow margin.

Jaruzelski votes in a national referendum held in 1987 on the question of whether to institute austerity measures aimed at curing Poland's economic ills. The government's program was rejected by the Polish people, but some of the measures were instituted anyway.

Poland, however, has peculiar election rules, which define a majority as 51 percent of eligible voters. A majority of the voters who participated in the referendum voted for approval, as Jaruzelski was quick to point out. The government, as it had said it would, raised prices anyway, although not as much as it would have if the reform program had not been approved. Even so, the increases were substantial; prices of basic foods went up 40 percent in early 1988.

Poles were worried but seemed to accept the inevitability of higher prices. In 1988, Jaruzelski claimed that workers were beginning to understand

Members of the Independent Students' Association carry a banner reading "Jaruzelski Must Go!" in 1988. As prices soared in Polish food stores that year, workers and students, behind a new, more radical leadership than were the founders of Solidarity, organized strikes and protests throughout Poland.

Soviet leader Mikhail Gorbachev chats with students in 1987. Gorbachev's policies of *glasnost* (openness) and *perestroika* (restructuring) have had profound and far-reaching implications for all the people and governments in the Eastern bloc.

the need for price hikes, sacrifices, and hard work. "People today, even if they are unhappy with the current state of the economy and living conditions, see the situation in a fuller, more rational way than they did in the 1950s, 1960s, and 1970s," he said. Perhaps this is because the memories of martial law are still very vivid for them.

Following the price hikes, strikes broke out in Bydgoszcz, and from there spread to other parts of the country, including Gdansk, where workers demanded not only higher pay but the relegalization of Solidarity. It was the most serious labor unrest since Solidarity was banned. The strikes, which also took the Solidarity leadership by surprise, were led by a new, more radical generation of workers who were too young to have participated in the 1980 strikes. They saw little hope for the future and were dangerous precisely because they were motivated not so much by enthusiasm, as the workers had been in 1980, as by bitterness and desperation. Jaruzelski responded much more forcefully to the new wave of workers' protest. He used riot police, for example, to break a steel strike in Nowa Huta, in southern Poland. The occupation strike in Gdansk ended after nine days, when Lech Walesa urged the workers to declare a "truce, not a defeat" and leave the shipyard peacefully.

A young Pole hawks Solidarity propaganda on a Warsaw street. Many believe that the "once banned, now legal, though censored" labor union coalition and its supporters represent the only hope for Poland's future.

The strikes have been the modern equivalent of the 19th-century insurrections. Whereas their grandfathers rose up against the Russian Empire, Poles in recent decades gathered inside factories and shipyards in defiance of a Communist authority they considered no more Polish than the czarist authorities who ruled Poland until 1918. The striking workers were considered patriotic heroes, while Jaruzelski, who crushed their strikes, was seen as the oppressor.

Jaruzelski has always regarded himself as a patriotic Pole. Nothing has seemed to offend him more than insinuations that he is a "Russian in a Polish uniform," as he was called by then–U.S. defense secretary Caspar Weinberger after the imposition of martial law. However, Jaruzelski's definition of patriotism has changed: Hard work and perseverance, he believes, are what will save Poland. Indeed, he now considers his countrymen burdened by their romantic sense of patriotism.

"My generation was raised in a spirit which was firmly rooted in our history, but above all in the heroic chapters, those of war and martyrdom," Jaruzelski explained in 1988. "Frankly speaking, this is still evident today in the consciousness of Poles. I would even say that this distinguishes us in a fundamental way from many other societies, which treat their traditions more comprehensively. That is, they give equal consideration to the patriotic, heroic, military traditions and to the pragmatic, positivist traditions of economic development, science, and progress. It seems we have always lacked this. This is our weakness even today."

The strikes in April and May were followed by another wave of labor unrest in August, when coal miners in Katowice went on strike for higher pay and the return of Solidarity. They were soon joined by thousands of workers in other mines and factories. Solidarity leaders appealed for talks with the government to defuse the labor unrest, and when the government refused, they called a strike at the Gdansk shipyard. Jaruzelski called for a "courageous turnaround" to pull Poland out of its crisis.

At the end of the month the Communist party proposed holding talks between government and Solidarity leaders on introducing political and economic changes in Poland. Walesa persuaded striking workers all over the country to return to work.

Walesa insisted that the government agree to legalize the Solidarity trade union before beginning talks. The government was unwilling to do that, and the talks appeared stalled. Then, at a Communist party meeting in January 1989, Jaruzelski threatened to resign if the party did not adopt a resolution opening the way for the legalization of Solidarity. The resolution was bitterly opposed by many party members. Later that month, two pro-Solidarity priests were found dead, one from carbon monoxide asphyxiation after a fire broke out in his room and the other clearly a murder victim, but the government said their deaths had no political link.

In a bold move, Jaruzelski turned to Solidarity for help and stretched out his hand to men who only a few years before he had imprisoned on charges of attempting to overthrow the state. In 1989 he offered parliamentary seats to the opposition and, in an unexpected and startling development, allowed Solidarity to form the first non-Communist coalition government in the Soviet bloc. In August, Jaruzelski nominated Tadeusz Mazowiecki, a close adviser to Solidarity leader Lech Walesa, as Poland's prime minister. The appointment of Mazowiecki, a devout Catholic, also reflected the influence of the Catholic church in Poland.

The move toward democracy in Poland was made possible by changes in the Soviet Union. The Brezhnev Doctrine, which said the Soviet Union had a duty to intervene militarily in any Eastern European country to keep a loyal Communist government in power, had been replaced by Mikhail Gorbachev's programs of *glasnost* (openness) and *perestroika* (restructuring). The broad political liberalization that was taking place in the Soviet Union made Jaruzelski's job easier.

The roundtable talks between Solidarity and the government began in February, and a historic ac-

> *During the dozen or so years of my work as Minister of National Defense several million people have done their military service together. . . . I would like to treat this as a bond linking us together, a trust on which I count and which I need badly today.*
> —WOJCIECH JARUZELSKI
> in a speech before the Sejm after being named prime minister,
> February 12, 1981

cord was signed two months later. The government agreed to legalize Solidarity and give it a share of parliamentary power, while Solidarity agreed to participate in and support government efforts to reform the economy. The accords also called for the creation of a government headed by a strong president and including a two-chamber parliamentary system.

Elections to both houses of parliament were held in June 1989, and the Communist party was humiliated. Even party leaders who were running unopposed were defeated, including Prime Minister Rakowski and General Czeslaw Kiszczak, the interior minister who had represented the government in the roundtable talks, because voters crossed their names off the ballot, thereby preventing them from receiving the support of 50 percent of the electorate they needed for election.

The plan all along had been for Jaruzelski to become the new president, but after the elections he was faced with opposition from both sides. On one side were Poles who had not forgiven him for imposing martial law; there were demonstrations in the streets to protest his expected candidacy. On the other side were Communist conservatives who said Jaruzelski gave too much power to the opposition and blamed him for the party's humiliating defeat in the elections. Jaruzelski responded by saying he would not run for president. "When there is an obstacle to reconciliation, to uniting social forces, there is only one possible solution — even if that obstacle is Wojciech Jaruzelski," he said. A couple of weeks later, Jaruzelski was persuaded to re-

At a World War II memorial ceremony, President Jaruzelski is flanked by former Solidarity adviser Tadeusz Mazowiecki (left), who became Poland's prime minister on August 24, 1989, and Lech Walesa, who now plays an official role in Poland's national affairs. The saga of Solidarity continues with these three leaders playing the key roles.

verse his decision, and the next day the parliament elected him president by the narrowest margin possible in a carefully orchestrated vote.

After he was elected president, Jaruzelski stepped down as leader of the Communist party and was replaced as first secretary by Rakowski, one of his strongest allies in the Communist leadership. Since he became Poland's leader in 1981, Jaruzelski had changed titles but he had not given up power. As president he still controlled the government and the army. Under the new governmental system, the president is commander in chief of the armed forces and has ultimate responsibility for foreign relations and national defense. He can appoint a prime minister, dissolve parliament, and call new elections. The president, who may serve two 6-year terms, can also declare one 90-day state of emergency. Jaruzelski appointed a Solidarity adviser as prime minister to head the first non-Communist government in the Soviet bloc, but he insisted on reserving for the Communists the ministries of defense and interior, which control the army and police. The day-to-day management of the economy was left to Solidarity. Men such as Jacek Kuron and Adam Michnik, intellectuals who had been imprisoned for their political beliefs many times in the past two decades, were now members of the government. Michnik was elected senator and Kuron was named minister of labor.

When Jaruzelski and his new government set out to bring Poland together, the economy was still in a state of crisis. By 1989 the foreign debt had reached $40 billion, and Poland's outdated, inefficiently managed industries were virtually worthless. Inflation was running at an annual rate of more than 100 percent, and millions of Poles were still suffering from shortages of food, housing, and health care. But although the battle was not over, and in some ways was just beginning, Jaruzelski had come far in his search for ways to get Poland back on track. He had been Poland's leader through tumultuous times and survived, his power intact. The future of Poland is uncertain, but Jaruzelski intends to see his country through to prosperity.

I never stopped being proud that I am a Pole.
—WOJCIECH JARUZELSKI

Further Reading

Ascherson, Neal. *The Polish August: The Self-Limiting Revolution.* New York: Viking, 1982.

Ash, Timothy Garton. *The Polish Revolution: Solidarity.* New York: Scribners, 1984.

Bialecki, Ireneusz, et al., eds. *Crisis & Transition: Polish Society in the 1980s.* New York: St. Martin's, 1987.

Brumberg, Abraham, ed. *Poland: Genesis of a Revolution.* New York: Random House, 1983.

Davies, Norman. *God's Playground: A History of Poland.* 2 vols. New York: Columbia University Press, 1982.

———. *Heart of Europe: A Short History of Poland.* New York: Oxford University Press, 1986.

Dobbs, Michael. *Poland, Solidarity, Walesa.* New York: McGraw-Hill, 1981.

Hahn, Werner G. *Democracy in a Communist Party: Poland's Experience Since 1980.* New York: Columbia University Press, 1987.

Jaruzelski, Wojciech. *Selected Speeches.* Edited by Robert Maxwell. Elmsford, NY: Pergamon Press, 1985.

Kaufman, Michael T. *Mad Dreams, Saving Graces: Poland—A Nation in Conspiracy.* New York: Random House, 1989.

Kaye, Tony. *Lech Walesa.* New York: Chelsea House, 1989.

Pfeiffer, Christine. *Poland: Land of Freedom Fighters.* Minneapolis: Dillon, 1984.

Raina, Peter. *Poland 1981: Towards Social Renewal.* London: Allen & Unwin, 1985.

Ruane, Kevin. *The Polish Challenge.* New York: Parkwest Publications, 1982.

Sandak, Cass R. *Poland.* New York: Watts, 1986.

Steven, Stewart. *The Poles.* New York: Macmillan, 1982.

Walch, Timothy. *Pope John Paul II.* New York: Chelsea House, 1989.

Walesa, Lech. *A Way of Hope.* New York: Henry Holt, 1987.

Weschler, Lawrence. *The Passion of Poland: From Solidarity Through the State of War.* New York: Pantheon, 1984.

Chronology

July 6, 1923	Born Wojciech Jaruzelski in Kurow, Poland
1933	Attends Catholic secondary school in Warsaw
1939	Outbreak of World War II; Jaruzelski leaves school and flees with family to Lithuania
Aug. 23, 1939	Adolf Hitler and Joseph Stalin sign nonagression pact
Sept. 1939	Nazis attack Poland from the west; Britain and France declare war on Germany; Soviets advance on Poland from the east
1940–42	Jaruzelski and his family deported to a Soviet labor camp
1943	Enlists in the First Polish Army; studies Marxist theory at the Polish Officers' School in Ryazan, USSR; commands platoon in the Jan Henryk Dabrowski Second Infantry Division
Jan. 1945	Participates in the Soviet liberation of Warsaw
May 4, 1945	Commands unit that reaches the Elbe River and makes contact with U.S. Army; V-E Day is celebrated four days later
1947–49	Jaruzelski enters Higher Infantry School at Rembertow; promoted to rank of lieutenant colonel
1954–56	Named head of the Department of Military Academies, Schools, and Officers' Courses; promoted to chief of the Central Department of Battle Training; promoted to rank of general
1957–60	Commands 12th Mechanized Division of the People's Army in Sczecin
1960	Named head of Main Political Board of the Polish Armed Forces
1962	Appointed deputy minister of national defense
1965	Appointed chief of the general staff
1968	Named minister of national defense; promoted to three-star general
1970	Several workers are killed by police during a strike at the Lenin Shipyard in Gdansk
Dec. 1971	Jaruzelski is elected full member of the Party Political Bureau at the Sixth Party Congress
1973	Promoted to the rank of four-star general
Sept. 1980	The Polish trade union, Solidarity, establishes headquarters in Gdansk with Lech Walesa as chairman of the Temporary National Committee
Feb. 12, 1981	Jaruzelski appointed prime minister of Poland
Dec. 13, 1981	Declares martial law in Poland
July 21, 1983	Martial law is lifted
June 4, 1989	Free elections are held in Poland; Jaruzelski is elected to the new post of president

Index

Altai Mountains, 42
Anders, Wladyslaw, 45
Armia Krajowa (Home Army), 47
Auschwitz, 48
Austria, 37
Austro-Hungarian Empire, 26, 27
Baltic Sea, 16, 37
Belgium, 40
Belorussia, 27, 51
Belza, Wladyslaw, 28
Berling, Zygmunt, 46, 50
Bierut, Boleslaw, 62, 68
Bijsk, 42
Birkenau, 48
Blitzkrieg, 39
Bolsheviks, 27
Brezhnev, Leonid, 99, 105
Britain, 38, 39
British Expeditionary Force, 40
Budapest, 70
Bug River, 39, 46
Bydgoszcz, 87, 103
Bydgoszcz Crisis, 88
Catholicism and Catholic church, 35–36, 61, 63, 64, 65, 82–83
Central Committee, 75
Central Department of Battle Training, 70
Chamberlain, Neville, 38
Churchill, Winston, 52
Communist party, 17, 91, 96, 98–99
Concentration camps, 48
Consultative Council, 99–100
Council of State, 19, 96
Czechoslovakia, 16, 20, 37, 73, 99
Danzig, 37
Democratic party, 19
Department of Military Academies, 70
Dubček, Alexander, 73
Dunkirk, 40
East Prussia, 53
Elbe River, 51–52
English Channel, 40
Estonia, 41
First Polish Army, 46
Forefathers' Eve, 72
France, 39, 40
Gdansk, 14, 26, 37, 69, 74, 84, 86, 103, 104

Gdansk Agreement, 85
General Staff Academy, 56
German Wehrmacht, 40
Germany, 37, 39, 47–51
Gierek, Edward, 75–79, 85–86
Glasnost, 42, 105
Glemp, Józef, 100
Gniezno, 36
Gomulka, Wladyslaw, 62, 68–69, 71, 72, 74–76
Gorbachev, Mikhail, 42, 99
Gornicki, Wieslaw, 99
Grande Armée, 30
Great Depression, 33
Gypsies, 48
Higher Infantry School, 56
Hitler, Adolf, 37–39, 48, 51
Holocaust, 48
Home Army, 47–48, 49, 50
Hungary, 16, 70, 99
Inter-Factory Strike Committee (MKS), 85
Jan Henryk Dabrowski Second Infantry Division, 46
January Uprising of 1863, 26, 28, 31
Jaruzelski, Monika (daughter), 70
Jaruzelski, Teresa (sister), 25
Jaruzelski, Wanda Zaremba (mother), 28
Jaruzelski, Wladyslaw (father), 42, 43
Jaruzelski, Wladyslaw (great-grandfather), 26
Jaruzelski, Wojciech
  atheism of, 60–61
  as commander in chief, 96
  as Communist party leader, 91, 96, 98–99
  creates Consultative Council, 99–100
  declares general amnesty, 99
  as defense minister, 70–71, 73
  deportation during World War II, 41–43
  economic reform plan of, 99, 107
  education of, 32, 35–37, 56–57
  elected to presidency, 19–20, 106–107
  family background, 25–28, 32, 33, 35
  heroes of, 30–31
  joins army in World War II, 46–48, 51
  joins Communist party, 20, 57
  martial law and, 13–16, 91–96
  Marxism and, 57–60

military career, 20–21, 45–46, 55–56, 70
patriotism of, 25, 29–32, 104
people's attitude toward, 98, 104
personality of, 21–22
political career, 19–20
and Solidarity, 14–20, 83–91, 96–106
view of Russians, 21, 57–58
Jaruzelski, Wojciech (grandfather), 26–27, 31
Jaskólska, Barbara (wife), 70
Jews, 40, 48–49, 72
John Paul II, pope, 82–83
Kania, Stanislaw, 85, 86, 88, 91
Katowice, 104
Katyn Forest, 42
Kazimierz, 36
Khrushchev, Nikita, 67
Kiszczak, Czeslaw, 99, 106
Kommunist, 42
KOR, 81–82, 84, 85
Kowalczyk, Stanislaw, 86
Kraków, 26, 82
Kuron, Jacek, 73, 107
Kurów, 25, 28
Latvia, 41
Leipzig, 30
Lenin, Vladimir, 27
Lenin Shipyard, 14, 84, 85
Lithuania, 27, 37, 40, 41
Lódź, 53
LOT, 95
Lublin, 25, 26, 27, 39, 46, 48
Lublin Committee, 46
Luftwaffe, 39
Lvov, 26, 48
Majdanek, 48
Martial law, 13–16, 91, 93, 96
Marx, Karl, 46, 59, 60
Marxism, 57–60
Mazowiecki, Tadeusz, 105
Michnik, Adam, 73, 81, 107
Mickiewicz, Adam, 22, 72
Mutual-assistance pacts, 41
Nagy, Imre, 69
National Coordinating Committee of the New Independent Self-governing Trades Union (NSZZ), 85

National theater, 72
Nations, Battle of the, 30
Nazi-Soviet Non-Aggression Pact (1939), 39, 61
Netherlands, 40
Ninth Party Congress, 89
Novak, Zrnka, 31, 55, 61
Ochab, Edward, 73
Oder River, 52
Oranienburg-Sachsenhausen, 48
Party Congress, 99
Peasant party, 19
Perestroika, 105
Pétain, Philippe, 40
Pilsudski, Józef, 27
Pinkowski, Józef, 85–86
Polish Committee of National Liberation (PKWN), 46
Polish Corridor, 37–38
Polish Officers' School, 46
Polish-Soviet War of 1919–20, 28
Polish United Workers party, 10
Politburo, 75, 83, 85, 99
Pomerania, 53
Pomeranian Wall, 51
Pommernstellung, 51
Pomozemy, 76
Poniatowski, Józef, 30–31
Popieluszko, Jerzy, 97
Powazki, 51
Poznan (Posen), 26
Praga, 50
Radom, 81
Rakowski, Mieczyslaw, 86, 88, 91, 99
Rembertow, 56
Riga, Treaty of, 28
Roosevelt, Franklin, 52
Rural Solidarity, 87
Russian Empire, 26
Russian Revolution, 27
Ryazan, 46
Sandomierz, 36
San River, 39
Schleswig-Holstein, 39
Sejm, 19, 73, 86, 91
Siberia, 41
Silesia, 53, 75
Smolensk, 42

111

Solidarity, 14–20, 83–91, 96–106
Solidarność, 84
Soviet NKVD, 41
Soviet Union, 15–16, 23, 38–39, 41, 42, 52, 55, 105
Spychalski, Marian, 73
Stalin, Joseph, 39, 45, 52, 58, 61, 62, 65, 67
Stalingrad, 46
Stalinism, 62–65, 67, 69
Szczecin, 70
Tabor, 27
Traugutt, Romuald, 30, 31
12th Mechanized Division, 70
Ukraine, 27
United Nations General Assembly, 99
University of Warsaw, 72
Ursus tractor factory, 81
Versailles, Treaty of, 37
Vistula River, 36, 50
Voroshylov Military Academy, 56
Walesa, Lech, 84, 86, 88, 100, 103, 105
Warsaw, 13, 25, 26, 37, 39, 49–51, 56, 68, 72, 100
Warsaw Pact, 70, 73, 88
Weinberger, Caspar, 104
Westerplatte, 39
Whitehead, John, 100
Wilno, 41, 47
Wola, 37
Workers Defense Committee, 81–82, 84, 85
World War I, 27, 32, 33, 37
World War II, 32, 37–53
Wyszynski, Stefan, 82
Yalta, 52
Zolibórz, 51

Lynn Berry holds an M.A. in Slavic languages and literature and a certificate in Russian and East European area studies from Indiana University. She has traveled in the Soviet Union and other European countries, including Poland, where she lived from 1984 to 1986 while on a graduate research fellowship at Warsaw University. She is currently employed at the Philadelphia bureau of the Associated Press.

Arthur M. Schlesinger, jr., taught history at Harvard for many years and is currently Albert Schweitzer Professor of the Humanities at City University of New York. He is the author of numerous highly praised works in American history and has twice been awarded the Pulitzer Prize. He served in the White House as special assistant to Presidents Kennedy and Johnson.

PICTURE CREDITS

Anonymous: p. 83; AP/Wide World: pp. 40, 41, 42, 46, 50, 64–65, 71, 74, 103, 106; Bettmann: pp. 26, 29, 31, 43, 44; Jan Hausbrandt: pp. 16, 80, 82, 87, 88, 90, 92, 94, 95, 100; Laski/SIPA: pp. 17, 20, 34, 56, 66, 78, 81, 84, 89, 97, 98, 101; Library of Congress: pp. 30, 32, 33, 54, 59; Malanca/SIPA: p. 21; Nadal/SIPA: p. 18; Courtesy of NZS (Independent Student Association, Poland): p. 102; Photoreport/SIPA: p. 69; Reuters/Bettmann: p. 2; Samobzielny Zespol Studiow: pp. 23, 24, 51, 72, 77; Setboun/SIPA: p. 75; Sipa-Press: pp. 12, 15; Maciek Szymczak: p. 104; UPI/Bettmann: pp. 27, 28, 36, 37, 38, 39, 47, 48, 49, 53, 60, 63, 70